D1308011

A
WINDOW
TO THE
PAST

A
WINDOW
TO THE
PAST

A Photographic Panorama of Early Church History and the Doctrine and Covenants

RICHARD NEITZEL HOLZAPFEL
and T. JEFFERY COTTLE

BOOKCRAFT

Salt Lake City, Utah

Copyright © 1993 by Bookcraft, Inc.

All rights reserved. No part of this book may be reproduced in any form or by any means without permission in writing from the publisher, Bookcraft, Inc., 1848 West 2300 South, Salt Lake City, Utah 84119.

Bookcraft is a registered trademark of Bookcraft, Inc.

Library of Congress Catalog Card Number: 92-75253
ISBN 0-88494-866-8

First Printing, 1993

Printed in the United States of America

For
Nathan, Zac, and Bailey Holzapfel
and for
Mike, Mark, and Jim Cottle

CONTENTS

Acknowledgments ix

Introduction 1

SECTION ONE: EARLY LATTER-DAY SAINT TEMPLES 3

Independence Temple 4

Far West Temple 6

Kirtland Temple 8

Nauvoo Temple 10

SECTION TWO: SOCIAL SETTINGS IN EARLY CHURCH HISTORY 13

Establishing a Home 14

Printing and Publishing 17

Women and Children 20

Music and Worship 23

Village and Family Life 25

Banking and Economics 27

Transportation 30

Frontier Life and Amusements 33

Clothing and Textiles 35

Communication and News 37

Missionaries 39

Food and Medicine 41

Military and Weapons 44

Lamanites 46

Courts and Jails 48

Writings, Records, and Books 50

Mercantile 52

Architects, Builders, and Craftsmen 54

Death and Burial 56

Photography and Art.. 58

Pioneers and Trails 60

SECTION THREE: THE DOCTRINE AND COVENANTS IN CHURCH HISTORY... 63

The Development of the Doctrine and Covenants 65

Commandments in the Doctrine and Covenants.................................. 73

The Joseph Smith Translation and the Doctrine and Covenants 75

The Nature of Revelation in the Doctrine and Covenants..................... 78

Geographic Locations of the Revelations 80

Select Bibliography 95

Sources of Photographs/Artifacts 97

ACKNOWLEDGMENTS

Without the assistance and cooperation of many individuals and institutions, this work would not have been possible. We acknowledge the help of several individuals, including Donald Albro, Harold Allen, Ronald Barney, Rick Boomgarden, Greg Christofferson, Gary Cottle, Michaela Voss Cottle, Larry Draper, Tyler Edmundsen, David Ettinger, Chad Flake, Jeni Broberg Holzapfel, D. J. Isom, Edith Menna, Melissa Ostler, Lee Pement, Ronald Read, Margaret Rich, Ronald Romig, Dana Roper, Roseline Seaver, Elbert Sheppard, R. Q. Shupe, William Slaughter, Steven Sorensen, Eldred G. Smith, Ted D. Stoddard, Richard Turley, and Alan Wood. We express gratitude also to our publisher, Bookcraft, Inc., who considered our proposal a valuable project—in particular, we thank Jana Erickson and Cinda Morgan for their extra efforts in the design and layout of the book.

Several institutions and the Eldred G. Smith family have graciously provided copies of photographs, access to artifacts within their collections, and permission to reproduce them. We thank the Archives Division, Church Historical Department, The Church of Jesus Christ of Latter-day Saints, Salt Lake City, Utah; Archives-Library, Missouri Historical Society, St. Louis, Missouri; British Museum, London, England; Cincinnati Public Library, Cincinnati, Ohio; Detroit Institute of the Arts, Detroit, Michigan; George Eastman House, International Museum of Photography, Rochester, New York; Illinois State Historical Library, Springfield, Illinois; Library-Archives and Museum, Reorganized Church of Jesus Christ of Latter Day Saints, Independence, Missouri; Library of Congress, Washington, D.C.; Manuscript Department, Special Collections, and Photoarchives, Harold B. Lee Library, Brigham Young University, Provo, Utah; Mariners Museum, Newport News, Virginia; Missouri State Historical Society, Columbia, Missouri; Museum of Church History and Art, The Church of Jesus Christ of Latter-day Saints, Salt Lake City, Utah; National Maritime Museum, Greenwich, England; National Society Daughters of Utah Pioneers Memorial Museum, Salt Lake City, Utah; Nauvoo Historical Society, Nauvoo, Illinois; Restoration Trails Foundation, Independence, Missouri; Special Collections, J. Willard Marriott Library, University of Utah, Salt Lake City, Utah; Smithsonian Institute, Washington, D.C.; Visual Resources Library, The Church of Jesus Christ of Latter-day Saints, Salt Lake City, Utah; Western Reserve Historical Society, Cleveland, Ohio; and the staffs at the Joseph Smith Historic Center, the LDS Visitors' Center, and Nauvoo Restoration, Inc., in Nauvoo, Illinois.

INTRODUCTION

As we consider the rich heritage we have received as Latter-day Saints and the faith and sacrifice of those who have gone before us, there is no question that the Lord blessed the early Saints of this dispensation, who were given "power to lay the foundation of this church, and to bring it forth out of obscurity and out of darkness" (D&C 1:30). Since its organization on 6 April 1830, The Church of Jesus Christ of Latter-day Saints has attracted a great host of converts and received much attention from the general public. In 1852, Charles Mackay, an English author, published a small engraved work that he claimed was the first public history of "that new religion" founded in America by Joseph Smith, Jr. (1805–1844), "one of the most remarkable persons who has appeared on the stage of the world in modern times" (*The Mormons, or Latter-day Saints* [London: Office of National Illustrated Library, 1852], p. iv). While it is certain that Mackay was not the first to write a public history of the Latter-day Saints, he was undoubtedly correct when he stated that Joseph Smith was a remarkable person. The Saints agree that their Prophet was an exceptional and inspired leader, but both Latter-day Saint and non–Latter-day Saint historians have also generally recognized that the church he founded and the converts to it were also extraordinary. Clearly this history is worth retelling to each succeeding generation.

Since the book of scripture known as the Doctrine and Covenants is intimately tied to the early history of the restored Church, our work draws many of its themes and topics from the text of this modern witness of Christ. The 1981 edition of the Doctrine and Covenants contains 138 sections and 2 official declarations. Of these, 133 were received principally through the Prophet Joseph Smith. The 7 remaining sections and declarations were received or recorded by or under the direction of Oliver Cowdery, John Taylor, Brigham Young, Joseph F. Smith, Wilford Woodruff, and Spencer W. Kimball (see sections 102, 134, 135, 136, 138, Official Declarations 1 and 2).

These important revelations, commandments, letters, prayers, and inspired writings are recognized by the Latter-day Saints as "the will of the Lord, . . . the mind of the Lord, . . . the word of the Lord, . . . the voice of the Lord, and the power of God unto salvation" (D&C 64:4). Through the pages of the Doctrine and Covenants, the world of the dedicated women and men of the Church is uncovered as they attempted to understand their personal missions, especially as those missions related to the coming forth of the kingdom of God in the latter days.

This book is an attempt to reveal our common Latter-day Saint history in a new and exciting way. It does not follow the customary method of describing the story based on a strictly chronological review of dates, names, and places. It uses material culture—artifacts—as a means of visualizing social settings. Material culture research is both an old and a new discipline in the United States, yet it still has not won a wide following among historians. While the definition of the term *material culture* is debated among scholars, we use the term to mean "artifacts." (See Thomas J. Schlereth, "Material Culture and Cultural Research," in *Material Culture: A Research Guide,* ed. Thomas J. Schlereth [Lawrence: University Press of Kansas, 1985], pp. 3–7.)

Traditionally, historians of the Church have not used artifacts as evidence in their research. Few of them have examined carefully the triptych of human necessities—clothing, food, and shelter. (An exception is the recently completed work of Carma de Jong Anderson, "A Historical Overview of the Mormons and Their Clothing, 1840–1850" [Ph.D. diss., Brigham

Young University, 1992].) Artifacts of the past, nevertheless, have become important evidences in the documentation and interpretation of the American experience in the broader field of American history. John Demos's pioneering study *A Little Commonwealth: Family Life in Plymouth Colony* (New York: Oxford University Press, 1970) examines the colonial family of Plymouth in a specific American context. In the absence of the usual literary sources, Demos centered his research on domestic shelter and artifacts of the seventeenth-century Pilgrim community.

Like most Americans of the period, a large segment of the early Latter-day Saint membership left few literary records. For the majority of people, the primary historical record of their lives is not written but survives as data gathered about them or, as happens even more frequently, as objects made and used and finally discarded by them.

This study, then, begins to collect and reproduce the artifacts of the Restoration, gathered from sources associated with both The Church of Jesus Christ of Latter-day Saints (LDS) and the Reorganized Church of Jesus Christ of Latter Day Saints (RLDS). Many historical studies relating to the history of the restored Church, like the broader field of American history, tend to be written for fellow academic specialists or for a narrow group of university-educated and well-read members of the Church. Material culturists, on the other hand, have usually worked in a more diverse and decentralized institutional structure composed of museums, government agencies like the National Park Service, and state historical societies. Institution staff members at the Museum of Church History and Art (LDS), Restoration Trails Foundation (RLDS), Nauvoo Restoration, Inc. (LDS), and the RLDS Museum Department have all made contributions in the area of understanding material culture. In this connection, it is interesting to note a statement from Thomas J. Schlereth, graduate director of the American Studies Department at the University of Notre Dame: "It must be acknowledged that material culture studies, despite all the methodological creativity demonstrated by some of its most pioneering proponents, are still only beginning to explore the conceptual and analytical potential of this approach to historical study" (*Material Culture: A Research Guide*, p. 159).

This study was prepared with the general public in mind, not a narrow group of specialists. Therefore, detailed interpretations of the meaning of such artifacts will have to be explored in another forum. It is our hope that this publication will be used by a wide cross section of the Church as a means of appreciating the story of our past.

EARLY LATTER-DAY SAINT TEMPLES

IN AN EARLY revelation, the Lord commanded the Saints to "establish a house, even a house of prayer, a house of fasting, a house of faith, a house of learning, a house of glory, a house of order, a house of God" (D&C 88:119). The Lord promised the faithful Saints an endowment of power from on high in the special houses of God, or temples, that they built. Temple sites were designated in Ohio, Missouri, and Illinois during the first two decades of the Church's existence (1830–1846).

Of particular interest, however, is the site of the temple in Missouri. About this site the Lord spoke to his Prophet:

"Yea, the word of the Lord concerning his church, established in the last days for the restoration of his people, as he has spoken by the mouth of his prophets, and for the gathering of his saints to stand upon Mount Zion, which shall be the city of New Jerusalem.

"Which city shall be built, beginning at the temple lot, which is appointed by the finger of the Lord, in the western boundaries of the State of Missouri, and dedicated by the hand of Joseph Smith, Jun., and others with whom the Lord was well pleased.

"Verily this is the word of the Lord, that the city New Jerusalem shall be built by the gathering of the saints, beginning at this place, even the place of the temple, which temple shall be reared in this generation." (D&C 84:2–4.)

In 1831, Joseph had already placed a cornerstone for a future temple at the site in Independence, which city the Lord designated as the "center place" of Zion (D&C 57:3). Joseph sent a plat map of the city of Zion to the leaders of the Church in Jackson County, Missouri, in June 1833. Because of persecution, the Saints were unable to fulfill their vision of erecting a temple in Zion (see D&C 124:49). Undaunted, they poured their efforts into completing their first temple in Kirtland, Ohio.

Notable spiritual experiences followed the years of sacrifices when the first two temples were completed in Kirtland and Nauvoo. The Kirtland "Pentecostal" period began several weeks preceding the actual dedication of the temple and continued until the Saints removed to Far West, Missouri, in 1838. The same was true of the Nauvoo Temple. During the Spirit-filled eventful winter of 1845–46, five thousand Saints received their sacred blessings in the temple as they prepared for their exodus and eventual removal to the Great Basin.

Nauvoo Temple Donation Box.

INDEPENDENCE TEMPLE

IN SEPTEMBER 1830, Joseph Smith received a revelation calling Oliver Cowdery to "go unto the Lamanites and preach my gospel unto them" (D&C 28:8). Within a month, Peter Whitmer, Jr., Parley P. Pratt, and Ziba Peterson were also called (see D&C 30 and 32). Before their departure, they signed a statement pledging their loyalty to each other and to their mission, where they hoped "to rear up a pillar as a witness where the temple of God shall be built, in the glorious new Jerusalem" (letter of Ezra Booth to Reverend Ira Eddy, 24 November 1831, Nelson, Ohio,

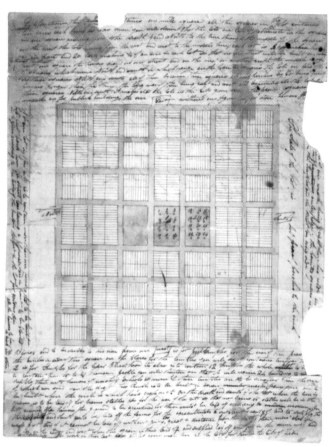

cited in the *Ohio Star*, 8 December 1831, published in Ravenna, Ohio). From the official founding of the Church in 1830 and throughout the next decade, Joseph Smith received several revelations that dealt with the location and building of a temple in Independence, Jackson County, Missouri. On 20 July 1831, the Lord said to Joseph, "Behold, the place which is now called Independence is the center place; and a spot for the temple is lying westward, upon a lot which is not far from the courthouse" (D&C 57:3). Sidney Rigdon was commanded to consecrate and dedicate the spot (D&C 58:57). Later, the Lord confirmed his command "that a house should be built unto me in the land of Zion, like unto the pattern which I have given you." The revelation further stated that the temple was to be built by "tithing and . . . sacrifice." (D&C 97:10–12.)

Independence (Zion) Plat Map. The Independence (Zion) plat map was the basic plat that leaders used for Mormon communities in Missouri, Illinois, and Utah. The temple was at the center of the plat—indicating the edifice's prominence in the community.

Temple Site Marker. The marker labeled "SECT 1831," which purportedly represents "South East Corner of the Temple 1831," may have been placed on 3 August 1831 after a reading of Psalm 87.

Newel K. Whitney's Map Containers.
On 25 June 1833, the Prophet Joseph Smith used the Newel K. Whitney map containers to send the plat map and other drawings to the Saints in Missouri from the Church headquarters in Kirtland. The containers undoubtedly also served other purposes.

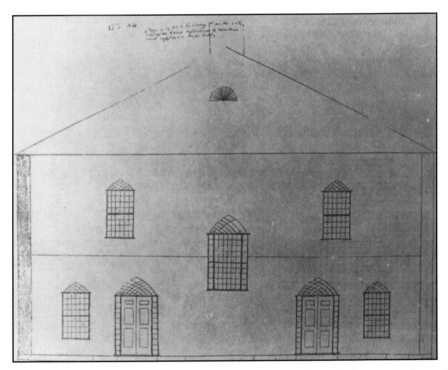

Independence Temple Drawing. Joseph Smith dedicated the temple lot in Independence, Missouri, on 3 August 1831. The site was purchased by Bishop Edward Partridge on 19 December 1831.

FAR WEST TEMPLE

A REVELATION GIVEN THROUGH Joseph Smith on 26 April 1838 announced that the city of Far West was to be a "holy and consecrated land" to the Lord (D&C 115:7). The Lord also enjoined the Saints to build up Far West as quickly as possible for the gathering of the Saints. He continued, "I command you to build a house unto me, for the gathering together of my saints, that they may worship me" (D&C 115:8). In July 1838, the Lord said of the Twelve Apostles: "Next spring let them depart to go over the great waters, and there promulgate my gospel, the fulness thereof, and bear record of my name." The revelation continued, "Let them take leave of my saints in the city of Far West, on the twenty-sixth day of April next, on the building-spot of my house, saith the Lord." (D&C 118:4–5.) Persecution and ultimately the Missouri governor's expulsion order prevented the Saints from erecting this temple.

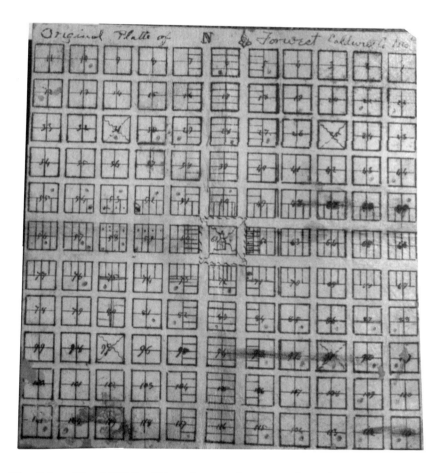

1838 Far West Plat Map. The 1838 Far West plat was drawn on sheepskin. The map shows the temple at the center of the city—illustrating the "City of Zion" concept that has been prominent in the Church since its days in Independence.

Far West Temple Cornerstone. In Doctrine and Covenants 115:7–8, the Lord commanded the Saints to build a temple at Far West. The cornerstones were finally laid at midnight on 26 April 1839. Many of the Twelve Apostles were present on that occasion.

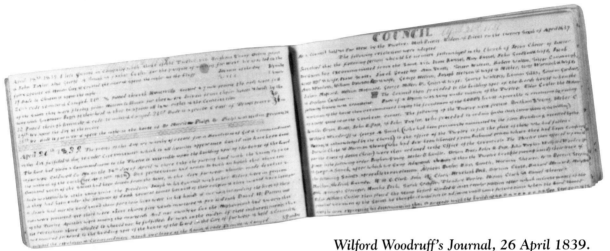

Wilford Woodruff's Journal, 26 April 1839.

In April 1839, Wilford Woodruff accompanied several Church leaders to Far West from the safety of Illinois. In an effort to avoid anti-Mormons in the area, the meeting on 26 April 1839, in which Wilford was ordained an Apostle, was held before daylight. Wilford was ordained while sitting on one of the temple cornerstones. The Apostles then began their missionary journey to the British Isles, thus fulfilling the revelation given a year earlier (see D&C 115).

Kirtland Temple

In a revelation to the Church, the Lord said: "And again, verily I say unto you, my friends, a commandment I give unto you, that ye shall commence a work of laying out and preparing a beginning and foundation of the city of the stake of Zion, here in the land of Kirtland, beginning at my house. And behold, it must be done according to the pattern which I have given unto you." (D&C 94:1–2.) Later, the Lord chastised the Saints for their slow progress on erecting the temple. "Ye must needs be chastened and stand rebuked before my face; for ye have sinned against me a very grievous sin, in that ye have not considered the great commandment in all things, that I have given unto you concerning the building of mine house" (D&C 95:2–3).

The Lord promised the "first elders" of the Church an "endowment from on high in my house, which I have commanded to be built unto my name in the land of Kirtland" (D&C 105:33). Eventually, a solemn cornerstone-laying ceremony on 23 July 1833 marked the commencement of the construction of the first completed Latter-day Saint temple. When the temple was finished in 1836, Joseph Smith offered a prayer of dedication (D&C 109); and a few days later he and Oliver Cowdery received in the temple a glorious vision of Jesus Christ, Moses, Elias, and Elijah (see D&C 110). The Spirit-filled days of this Pentecostal period began several weeks earlier when Joseph Smith and several brethren met on 21 January 1836 in the attic offices of the nearly completed temple. During this evening meeting Joseph Smith received a great vision of the celestial kingdom (see D&C 137).

Kirtland Temple. The Kirtland Temple measures 59 by 79 feet and is two and a half stories high. It is the first major structure erected by the Church—a monument of the devoted labor and sacrifice of the first thousand Church members.

Emer Harris's Square. The builders of the Kirtland Temple were skilled craftsmen. The temple was originally to have been built of brick but was finally built of stone from a nearby quarry. The exterior is made of solid stone covered with stucco plaster, and the interior includes beautiful woodworking exemplified by moldings, carvings, and the windows.

Kirtland Temple Window. The Kirtland Temple shows a mixture of styles. The main doorway, for example, exemplified the Federal style, while this is a Gothic window. The temple tower is a combination of Gothic and Greek architectural elements.

Temple Curtain Pulleys. The pulleys allowed the rollers at the auditorium's ceiling to lower curtains that subdivided the auditorium into several rooms.

West Pulpit of the Lower Assembly Room. The west pulpit of the lower assembly room is where the Lord Jesus Christ appeared to Joseph Smith and Oliver Cowdery to accept the temple. Moses, Elias, and Elijah also appeared during a series of visions. (See D&C 110.)

Kirtland Temple Step Stone. The temple foundation was made of smoothly cut stone, and the ends of the steps were finished with a vertical texture. The main walls, made of rough stone, were originally covered with white plaster, mixed with ground-up glass and china to make the plaster sparkle.

Nauvoo Temple

Following their expulsion from Missouri during the winter of 1838–39, the Saints began to gather on the western and eastern banks of the Mississippi River in Iowa and Illinois. After Joseph Smith regained his freedom from incarceration in Missouri, he settled in Commerce (later known as Nauvoo and the City of Joseph). In an important revelation dated 19 January 1841, the Lord commanded the Saints to bring their "gold, . . . silver, and . . . precious stones" to build in Nauvoo "a house to my name, for the Most High to dwell therein" (D&C 124:26–28).

The revelation had monumental significance to Joseph and other Church leaders because its fulfillment engaged nearly every waking moment of their time, not only until Joseph's death in 1844 but also until the Saints' final exodus from Nauvoo in 1846.

The temple ground-breaking occurred on 18 February 1841 when the basement for the temple was started. At the annual Church conference held on 6 April 1841, the First Presidency laid the four cornerstones. The main temple walls were only partially completed when Joseph and Hyrum Smith were murdered in 1844. Despite persecution and a knowledge that they would eventually evacuate the city, the Saints, under Brigham Young's direction, continued their efforts to complete the temple. By December 1845 the rooms in the temple attic were sufficiently completed to begin to administer the ordinances of the endowment. Later, temple sealings were also performed in the Nauvoo Temple. During an eight-week period, nearly six thousand Saints received their temple blessings in the Nauvoo Temple.

Nauvoo Temple Architect's Drawing. The temple architect, William Weeks, rendered this drawing of the Nauvoo Temple in ink and graphite on paper. This was the last of a series of drawings of the temple by Weeks. Joseph Smith, having received revelation on the matter, was responsible for the temple's design and general supervision, but Weeks drafted numerous sketches and drawings and handled the day-to-day construction problems. Weeks also designed the Nauvoo House, the Nauvoo Arsenal, and the Nauvoo Masonic Temple–Cultural Hall.

Alpheus Cutler's Building Tools.
Tools such as these were indispensable
in the stone construction of the temple.
They were used to both cut and form
the temple stone.

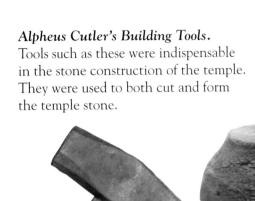

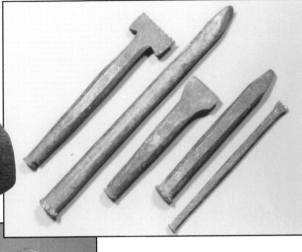

Nauvoo Temple Limestone.
The Nauvoo Temple was
built of gray limestone
(note the drill marks). The
interior was white pine,
similar in style to the first
Mormon temple in
Kirtland.

**Francis Clark's Spiral Template and
Drafting Tools.** Francis Clark was an
expert stonecutter, and he used drafting
tools and templates to draw and then
cut the patterns on the gray limestone
or interior wood of the Nauvoo Temple.

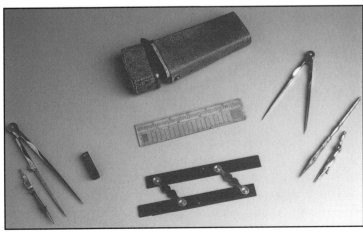

Part of Stone Oxen from Baptismal Font. Baptisms for the dead took place in the Nauvoo Temple baptismal font. The temple's first font was made of wood but eventually was replaced by a stone font.

Star Stone from the Nauvoo Temple. The temple walls were from four to six feet thick. The decoration of the outer wall included a moon stone, sun stone, and star stone representing the doctrine of the three degrees of glory revealed in Doctrine and Covenants section 76.

Nauvoo Temple Sacrament Cup. The Nauvoo Temple was used for many occasions, including social events, quorum meetings, sacrament meetings, and temple ordinances. In Nauvoo, the Saints did not construct meetinghouses. For large public meetings, the Saints used groves, boweries, and, finally, the temple.

Thomas Easterly's Daguerreotype of the Temple. The Nauvoo Temple was finally dedicated in a special night service on 30 April 1846. The temple cost over one million dollars and represented an incredible accomplishment for the Saints.

Nauvoo Temple Key. The principal and possibly the only entrance to the temple was through the west doors.

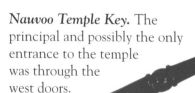

Apparently there were ten large stone steps leading to this entrance. The keys for the temple were hand cast and filed and polished.

SOCIAL SETTINGS IN EARLY CHURCH HISTORY

AN ABUNDANCE OF physical artifacts remains from the nineteenth century—homes and buildings (including foundations and architectural plans), furniture, tools, utensils, clothing, and the like. From the Latter-day Saints and their communities, a surprising number of artifacts have survived the rigors of pioneer life and travel, early persecution, and natural loss. The items included in this section represent a small portion of the material culture still available today. They help us visualize the world of the early Saints—a world that is increasingly lost to us in a modern technological setting.

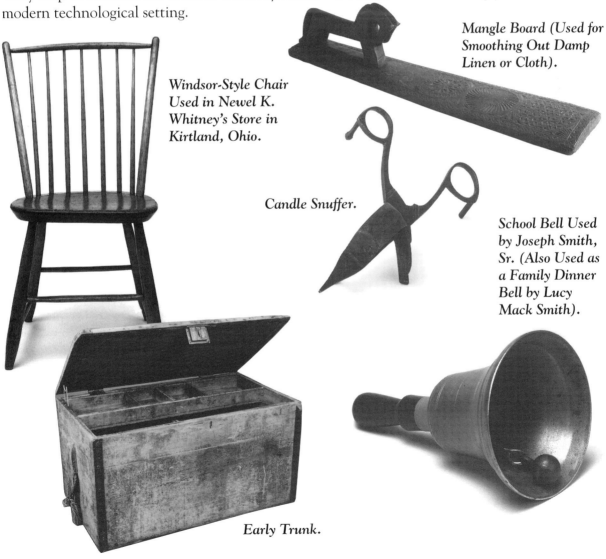

Mangle Board (Used for Smoothing Out Damp Linen or Cloth).

Windsor-Style Chair Used in Newel K. Whitney's Store in Kirtland, Ohio.

Candle Snuffer.

School Bell Used by Joseph Smith, Sr. (Also Used as a Family Dinner Bell by Lucy Mack Smith).

Early Trunk.

ESTABLISHING A HOME

MANY OF THE SAINTS established more than one home in a ten-year period (1830–1840). The Saints from New England and New York gathered to Ohio pursuant to Doctrine and Covenants sections 37 and 38, and then to Missouri according to sections 57, 58, and 59. Persecution next forced the Saints to relocate in northern Missouri and finally in Illinois and Iowa (see sections 124 and 125).

The first Joseph Smith, Sr., home in New York was a log cabin near what would come to be known as the Sacred Grove, where in the spring of 1820 the Father and the Son appeared to young Joseph in response to his prayer. Following the First Vision, the Smith family continued to reside in the log cabin, where the angel Moroni appeared to Joseph in 1823. The home was a one-and-one-half-story structure with a twenty-four-foot by thirty-foot foundation. The space in the home was used completely. The ground floor was divided into two rooms, and the attic was also sectioned into two separate areas.

The Smith's stay in the Manchester area depicts the typical four-stage development of an early nineteenth-century farm. First, enough timber was cleared to erect a log cabin. Second, fences, crops, and a kitchen garden were established. Third, a barn, other outbuildings, an expanded house, and an orchard were added. Fourth, a new plank or brick house was erected. From this early home until Joseph Smith, Jr., moved into the Mansion House in Nauvoo, the range and variety of buildings in Mormon communities were extremely vast.

Joseph Smith's Axe Head. Joseph Smith's axe head is forged from a single piece of metal. An axe was an essential tool of the early Saints. It served to clear the land, provide logs and cut notches in building log cabins, and cut wood for the cabin fireplace and for fences. Fences were necessary for keeping some animals in and other animals out. Rail fences were the most popular. Good neighbors built stiles, or steps, into their fences so people could easily get over the fences. Settlers often walked across each other's property because doing so was the shortest distance to the village or mill.

Howard and Martha Knowlton Coray's Log Cabin. The log cabin of Howard and Martha Knowlton Coray was typical of cabins at the time. Logs were usually felled and cut to a uniform length. Notches were made in both ends, and the logs were laid into position. Moss, mud, leaves, or plaster were used to fill in the space between the logs. The roof of the cabin was made of smaller logs and pieces of bark and later was usually replaced with shingles.

Fireplace Swing Crane. A fireplace swing crane was attached to the back of the fireplace and was made to swing out from the hearth so that the pots could be more easily stirred. Immediately after the cabin was under way, the fireplace was started. The foundation was built up with stones, and the chimney was erected. The hearth was then made. Because the fireplace provided light, warmth, and heat for cooking, the family's indoor activities revolved around the fireplace. The fire was usually kept burning night and day because of the difficulty of lighting a fire.

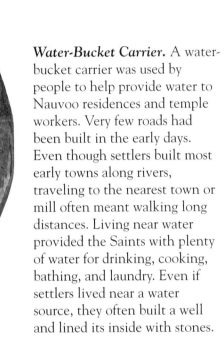

Water-Bucket Carrier. A water-bucket carrier was used by people to help provide water to Nauvoo residences and temple workers. Very few roads had been built in the early days. Even though settlers built most early towns along rivers, traveling to the nearest town or mill often meant walking long distances. Living near water provided the Saints with plenty of water for drinking, cooking, bathing, and laundry. Even if settlers lived near a water source, they often built a well and lined its inside with stones.

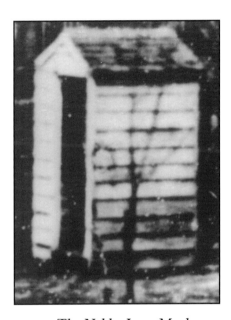

The Noble–Lucy Mack Smith Home Latrine. After building a log cabin or house, the settlers next began constructing outbuildings. An outhouse and barn were usually the first buildings to be added. These latrines also served for trash disposal. Hotels often had double latrines for use by both males and females. Chamber pots were kept near the bed for late-night emergencies.

Nauvoo Pitcher. The settlers used a pitcher and basin daily to wash their faces and hands. A pitcher usually stood waiting for use. Small wooden tubs were often used to bathe children.

A Stool Used in the Smith Family Cabin. The stool from the Smith family cabin was probably kept in the "best room," or parlor. The parlor was a special room in the home where guests were entertained. The best furniture was placed in this room. Here also the needlework was done, courting took place, and on Sundays the family gathered to read the Bible together.

Wood and Rope Bed. The early settlers slept in beds of wood and rope. The frame and legs were carved from wood. Holes were then bored in the four sides of the frames. Rope was pulled through the holes to make a net. A mattress of straw, corn husks, hay, boughs, or goose feathers was placed on top of this rope net. (Some mattresses contained straw on one side, which was cool in the summer, and goose feathers on the other side, which was warm in the winter.) The weight of the persons sleeping in the bed eventually caused the net to sag, and it had to be tightened from time to time. Several types of beds were used, some of which were particularly beneficial in saving space. Trundle beds, which were low beds on wheels, could be pushed under higher beds. Turn-up beds, which were built into the walls and could be raised during the day, were also used.

PRINTING AND PUBLISHING

As communities such as Palmyra grew, the need for information became important. A printer published newspapers, religious pamphlets, almanacs, schoolbooks, and government papers. All of the letters used in a word were handmade out of metal. These letters were called matrixes. Matrixes were stored in a wooden frame called a composition. The composition housed trays of letters of various type sizes and styles for use in the printer's work. The process from composing the words and lines to the finished product was long and tedious. Newspapers were easier to make than books. When the pages of a book were finished, a bookbinder bound them together by hand.

Following the publication of the Book of Mormon, the Lord commanded Martin Harris to "pay the debt thou hast contracted with the printer" (D&C 19:35). Eventually, William W. Phelps was called to be the first Church printer (see D&C 57:11). The Literary Firm, organized in November 1831, was commissioned to print all the official literature of the Church (see D&C 70). Included in the plans of the firm was the printing of Joseph Smith's translation of the Bible, Church hymnals, Church almanacs, children's literature, and Church newspapers. Printing and publishing thus played a significant role in spreading the message of the Restoration.

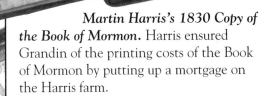

Martin Harris's 1830 Copy of the Book of Mormon. Harris ensured Grandin of the printing costs of the Book of Mormon by putting up a mortgage on the Harris farm.

Inkwell. Quill and ink were used by Joseph's scribes in producing the Book of Mormon manuscript.

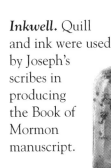

The Grandin Print Shop. E. B. Grandin bought his Palmyra printing business and bookstore in 1827 from John H. Gilbert. The Book of Mormon was printed on the third floor, the book bindery was on the second floor, and a bookstore occupied the first floor.

Grandin's "Smith Patented Improved Press." The printing press Grandin used became available in 1824 and was used in the Grandin printing establishment to print the first edition of the Book of Mormon. The work of hand setting the type began in August 1829; by 26 March 1830, the book had been printed and bound.

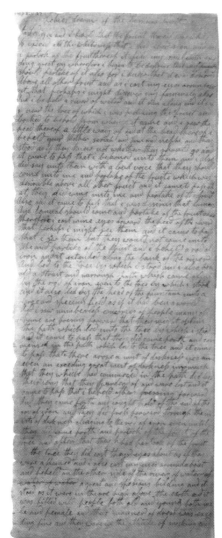

Original Manuscript of the Book of Mormon. The section shown contains Lehi's vision of the tree of life located in 1 Nephi 8. This was the manuscript the scribes wrote as Joseph Smith dictated the record contained on the gold plates. Many of the early revelations in the Doctrine and Covenants (see sections 3, 5, 6, 7, 8, 11, 12, and 13) concern issues raised while Joseph Smith and Oliver Cowdery translated the Book of Mormon.

Printer's Copy of the Manuscript of the Book of Mormon. Because of hostility in Palmyra and Martin Harris's loss of the first one hundred sixteen pages of the translation, Joseph Smith requested that Oliver Cowdery recopy the entire manuscript for the printer. Neither manuscript was punctuated. After Oliver completed recopying the manuscript in August 1829, he delivered the first twenty-four pages to Grandin's print shop.

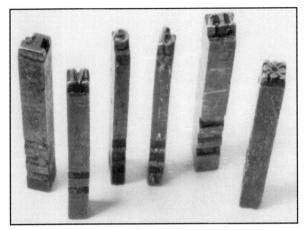

Type from the Grandin Printing Shop. Early printing required the type for each sheet to be inked separately. Leather ink balls served this function. Approximately three hundred pieces of type were recovered from the Grandin printing shop. The typeface known as Duodecimo was used for the Book of Mormon. Printing the Book of Mormon was a difficult process. Each individual type character had to be picked out of the type case (the capital letters were in the upper type drawer, or case, and regular type in the lower type case; hence, our designations of upper and lower case). A normal print order in the 1830s was five hundred to one thousand copies, so the Book of Mormon was a very lengthy project, as it consisted of three thousand copies. The job required extremely long hours of labor from numerous printers and helpers.

Printer Page Proof Sheet. Pictured is the first printer's page proof sheet from the Book of Mormon. When the title page proof sheet was printed at Grandin's, Joseph Smith, Jr., Joseph Smith, Sr., Hyrum Smith, Oliver Cowdery, and Martin Harris were present. They all examined and passed the proof sheet from hand to hand and "pronounced it good."

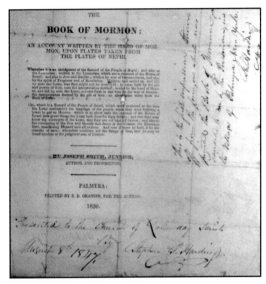

Signature of the Book of Mormon. A book is printed in "signatures," or groups of from eight to thirty-two pages printed front and back. The signatures are then folded to produce a book.

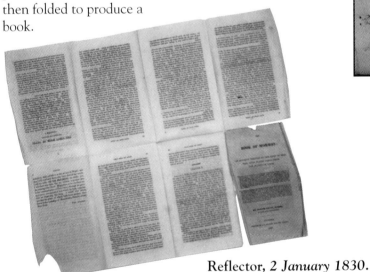

Reflector, 2 January 1830.
On 2 September 1829, Abner Cole began publishing a weekly newspaper in Palmyra called the *Reflector.* Cole used the pseudonym "O. Dogberry" in publishing the weekly from the Grandin printing establishment. Cole started to print sections of the Book of Mormon in the *Reflector* without permission, beginning with the 2 January 1830 issue. After a confrontation between Cole and Joseph Smith, Cole eventually stopped printing extracts from the Book of Mormon in his paper.

WOMEN AND CHILDREN

THE DOCTRINE AND COVENANTS speaks of women as daughters, wives, mothers, and widows. The Lord called Vienna Jaques and Emma Smith "handmaids" (see D&C 90:28; 132:51). The Lord reminded the men of the Church: "Love thy wife with all thy heart, and . . . cleave unto her and none else" (D&C 42:22). The wives, while copartners with their spouses, nevertheless had "claim on their husbands for their maintenance" (D&C 83:2).

The Lord also reminded parents that "children have claim upon their parents for their maintenance" (D&C 83:4). Furthermore, parents were expected to teach their children basic gospel principles (see D&C 68:25). By and large, this responsibility was fulfilled by the wife and mother of the family—but it was not the only aspect of the woman's sphere in the early Church.

Sister Saints played a vital role in the early Mormon gathering places of Ohio, Missouri (Independence, Adam-ondi-Ahman, and Far West), and Nauvoo. They did much to found, build, and maintain their communities while the men were away serving Church missions and participating in business and political activities.

When the Lord commanded the Saints to build a temple in Nauvoo, he asked the Saints to bring "your gold, and your silver, and your precious stones" to help finish the temple (D&C 124:26). The sister Saints of Nauvoo, while performing their traditional duties as wives and mothers, also helped in many significant and practical ways to complete the building. The women's sphere increased with the formation of the Female Relief Society in 1842 and the restoration of ancient temple covenants.

Baby Clothes, Socks, Cap, and Cradle. Besides managing the home and preparing the family meals, a woman's most important task was childbearing and childrearing. Childbearing posed a high risk to the mother's health and life and was also extremely taxing emotionally because of the high mortality rate of infants and children.

Marbles and Doll Used in Nauvoo. Children's favorite pastimes were playing with dolls and marbles. Numerous types of dolls were available, ranging from simple rag dolls to fine porcelain dolls. Marbles were made out of clay or porcelain and later out of glass. Children played many different games with marbles, games with names such as "circles," "follow on," and "single hole."

Rocking Horse Used by the Saints' Children in Nauvoo. Real horse hair was used for the mane and tail of this expertly crafted rocking horse. Despite the often rugged and challenging conditions of frontier life, parents and craftsmen nevertheless took care to provide children with beautiful toys made with great artistry and love.

Slate Tablet and Slate Pencil. Education was a luxury that many early settlers could not afford. Within the Mormon community, education was highly valued and encouraged. Many of the books the students studied were of a religious nature. The first schoolhouses had dirt floors and paper windows. Although school was important, children began to help around the home and to work at a young age. They were given a number of duties, such as collecting berries, taking care of small domestic animals, making candles, or even driving a team of horses.

Candle Maker Used in Nauvoo. Candle making was an extremely messy process. Candle molds were made of pewter or tin. To make candles, settlers boiled animal and vegetable fat to remove the water and then skimmed off the dirt, leaving a material called tallow. Burning these candles released a smell of fried grease. Making candles, soap, clothes, butter, and bread represented only a few of the time-consuming chores expected of women and their children on the frontier.

Perfume Bottle from Nauvoo, Cosmetic Container, and Gold Bead from a Necklace. The gold bead belonged to Emma Smith. The sister Saints in Nauvoo owned some elegant accessories, but these items were probably used only on special occasions.

Relief Society Donation Box, Pennies, Nails, and Temple Glass. Women were often involved in charitable activities. The Relief Society used this wooden caddy to collect pennies in an effort to buy nails and glass for the Nauvoo Temple.

MUSIC AND WORSHIP

AN IMPORTANT REVELATION to Emma Smith noted, "For my soul delighteth in the song of the heart; yea, the song of the righteous is a prayer unto me, and it shall be answered with a blessing upon their heads" (D&C 25:12). Music was an important part of family and community life in America from the earliest colonial times. It also played a significant role in the church services of the early Saints. Emma Smith was given the assignment to collect sacred songs for the Church, and a hymnal was published in 1835.

The early Church's worship services included the administration of the sacrament. Priesthood bearers performed this duty (see D&C 20:38–40, 46, 58) in a manner prescribed by revelation (see 20:75–79). The Lord commanded the Saints that when they assembled they should "instruct and edify each other" (D&C 43:8). The Lord specified that Sunday should be a sacred and holy day that included fasting and prayer (D&C 59:12–14). Also, special blessing meetings for the Saints were presided over by the Patriarch to the Church.

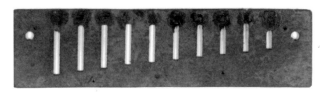

Harmonica Plate from Nauvoo. Music was a valued part of the Saints' life. When the daily work was done, the saints attended dances and band performances. Most of the musical instruments came from Europe, although simple instruments like the harmonica could be produced locally. Sometimes cabinet makers crafted pianos, harpsichords, and spinets.

Clarinet. Artisans who manufactured musical instruments such as this in America sometimes had a difficult time making a living because so much time was required to make one instrument. Many times, these artisans had to farm or to do other work on the side.

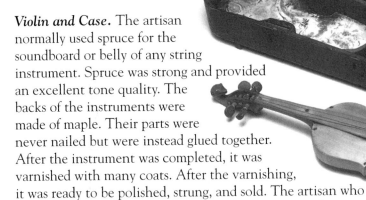

Violin and Case. The artisan normally used spruce for the soundboard or belly of any string instrument. Spruce was strong and provided an excellent tone quality. The backs of the instruments were made of maple. Their parts were never nailed but were instead glued together. After the instrument was completed, it was varnished with many coats. After the varnishing, it was ready to be polished, strung, and sold. The artisan who created the pictured violin carved a unique head on the instrument.

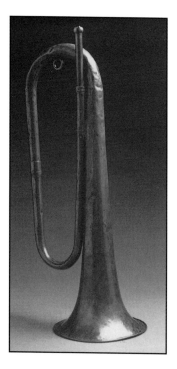

Bugle. The Saints had a brass band in Nauvoo. The instruments played by the band included trumpets, French horns, clarinets, bugles, trombones, and bass drums.

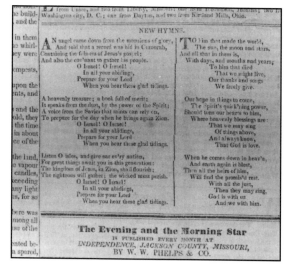

The Evening and the Morning Star. Before 1835, the *Star* started publishing hymns selected by Emma Smith consequent upon her calling from the Lord as recorded in Doctrine and Covenants 25:11.

Pewter Sacrament Cup Used in Nauvoo. The administration of the sacrament was an important part of any early Church worship service. In addition to regular services on the Sabbath, local prayer and blessing meetings were held in intimate home settings with neighbors, even in Nauvoo.

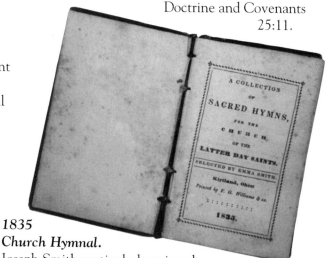

1835 Church Hymnal. Joseph Smith particularly enjoyed music and always encouraged music in Kirtland, Missouri, and Nauvoo. The Saints received great pleasure in singing traditional religious music, but the new faith needed its own hymns to express its doctrines. Besides the music at public occasions, religious meetings, holidays, and weddings, the Saints often sang hymns at partings and at departures for missions.

Cello and Bow. Musical instruments like the cello and violin needed to be made of wood from carefully chosen trees. The best trees were actually those grown in the worst soils. These trees grew stronger because of minerals contained in the soil. An artisan could identify such wood because when it was hit with an axe, the wood seemed to "sing." Apprentices to such musical instrument artisans were taught how to find the trees that sang. Such trees produced blocks of wood that were then aged before the instruments were crafted.

VILLAGE AND FAMILY LIFE

THE DOCTRINE AND COVENANTS frequently mentions family matters and community responsibilities (see D&C 20:47, 51; 52:36; 75:28; 93:48; and 134). A feeling of community developed in an area as the population grew.

Kirtland, located in the Western Reserve area of northeastern Ohio, was first settled in 1811. As the town grew, it was organized into a township in 1818. The Newel K. Whitney store was established in 1823. When the first Mormon missionaries arrived in October 1830, Kirtland was still a small community.

Individuals shared resources and assisted each other in large tasks, such as raising barns. As the Saints gathered to build their temple, religious commitment to the restored gospel added another dimension to village and family life. People trusted each other and relied on each other's honesty. Few locked their doors, and often a traveler could just walk into a home to find a place by the fire to rest. Life centered around the family and the daily duties of survival.

1838 Plat Map of Adam-ondi-Ahman (Missouri).
This map followed the model for all stakes of Zion. It was laid out on a north-south axis from the public building blocks that would have included the temple. The drafting of a plat map was evidence of the formation of a community.

Brigham Young's Wood Plainer, Ruler, and Promissory Note. As in most early communities, the Saints were always ready to help each other achieve a difficult task. Work parties allowed Saints to complete, in one or two days, tasks that required a single man months to accomplish. Lending was also common in early communities, particularly items like sugar, flour, medicine, and common tools.

Nauvoo Mansion House Rain Gutter. The tinsmiths were very important in the community because of the large variety of items they could produce, including kitchen wares, tools, and even rain gutters. Items such as these were usually obtained through the barter system. The sense of community or the feeling of an extended family was further enhanced by the barter system.

Chair Made by Brigham Young. As the community expanded, more and more village artisans produced goods. This included woodworkers. Some of the wood items available included a large assortment of furniture, such as desks, tables, trunks, and benches.

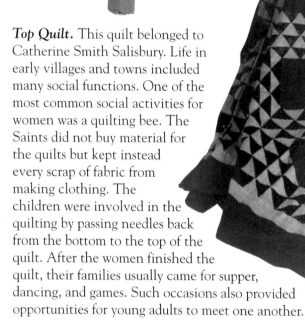

Top Quilt. This quilt belonged to Catherine Smith Salisbury. Life in early villages and towns included many social functions. One of the most common social activities for women was a quilting bee. The Saints did not buy material for the quilts but kept instead every scrap of fabric from making clothing. The children were involved in the quilting by passing needles back from the bottom to the top of the quilt. After the women finished the quilt, their families usually came for supper, dancing, and games. Such occasions also provided opportunities for young adults to meet one another.

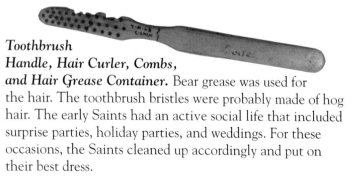

Toothbrush Handle, Hair Curler, Combs, and Hair Grease Container. Bear grease was used for the hair. The toothbrush bristles were probably made of hog hair. The early Saints had an active social life that included surprise parties, holiday parties, and weddings. For these occasions, the Saints cleaned up accordingly and put on their best dress.

Banking and Economics

THE LORD COMMANDED Martin Harris to "pay the debt" to E. B. Grandin for the publication of the first edition of the Book of Mormon (D&C 19:35). Several other revelations deal directly with economic matters (see D&C 64, 72, 104, 111, 115, and 119).

The Church and its members were part of a larger economic setting in the United States during the first decades following the founding of the Church. Economic considerations constantly plagued the Saints as they attempted to establish communities in Ohio, Missouri, and Illinois.

During a period when Church expenses had risen dramatically, several Kirtland community leaders established the Kirtland Safety Society. Several banks opened in nearby communities, and with the Church and individual members under financial pressure, the decision to start a bank was a logical one. When the state legislature denied the group a banking charter, an anti-bank company was formed. Within a short time of the company's opening, company officials suspended payment in hard currency; after legal maneuvering and difficulties, the company closed its doors in November 1837, during the 1837 financial crisis that plagued the entire nation.

While the Saints attempted to manage their temporal concerns, the Lord revealed "line upon line" concerning his own economic order—the law of consecration and stewardship. The Saints accepted this celestial law and sought to live by its principles on several occasions. The core of the law was revealed through Joseph Smith as a commandment that the Saints should "consecrate of thy properties for [the poor's] support that which thou hast to impart unto them, with a covenant and a deed which cannot be broken. And inasmuch as ye impart of your substance unto the poor, ye will do it unto me; and they shall be laid before the bishop of my church and his counselors, two of the elders, or high priests, such as he shall appoint or has appointed and set apart for that purpose." (D&C 42:30–31.)

Following almost a decade of challenges in keeping this law, the Lord gave the Saints the law of tithing (see headnote to D&C 119).

Kirtland Safety Society Bank.
Individual Saints in the 1830s had little need for a bank. The barter system worked particularly well for farmers and artisans. The general store usually acted as the community bank. The store lent seeds, tools, and wares to farmers, and the farmers settled their debts when their crops were harvested. In establishing a large community, however, with needs including transportation costs, land, publication costs, public works, and the building of a temple, the Saints had to establish a bank. Many surrounding communities smaller than Kirtland had banks. The Saints established a bank in 1836.

Kirtland Safety Society Bank Note. In part to help relieve Church leaders of the increasing debt the Church had encumbered, the Kirtland Safety Society opened for business during the first week of January 1837. Within the first few days of operation, the one-, two-, and three-dollar denominations began trading. Like any stock certificate or note not issued by the federal government, the bills' value and ability to be exchanged were vulnerable. If a note was redeemed and not reissued, often the word *canceled* was written across the note.

Kirtland Safety Society Anti-Bank Note.
When the state of Ohio refused to charter the Kirtland Bank, the bank officials decided to operate it as an anti-banking company. Wording modifications that reflected this change in name were stamped on those notes whose design could accommodate such modifications.

Period United States Coinage. These pieces of coinage include a half-dime, dime, fifty-cent piece, and dollar. They were in use in the 1820s to 1840s. Although gold was the preferred medium of exchange, these coins were more abundant.

Kirtland Safety Society Bank Iron Safe. The Saints could not obtain a bank charter from the Ohio legislature, so the proposed bank changed its form to an anti-bank. Joseph Smith purchased the safe on 18 October 1836.

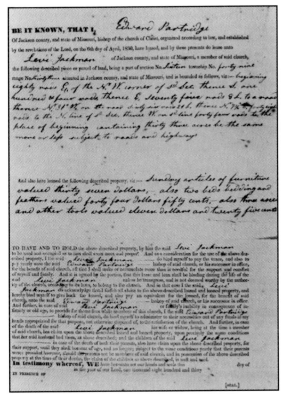

Early 1830s Stewardship Agreement. This stewardship lease is from Edward Partridge, called by revelation as first bishop of the Church (D&C 41:9). In Doctrine and Covenants sections 42 and 51, the Saints were placed under the law of consecration. They were asked to consecrate all their property to the bishop of the Church, who then was to grant them a stewardship over some or all of their properties based upon their circumstances, wants, and needs.

Nauvoo House Association Notes (First Issue). As a result of the revelation now designated as section 124 in the Doctrine and Covenants, the Saints issued stock certificates to build the Nauvoo House. Stock certificates were also issued for land companies, the Nauvoo Music Association, the Seventies, the Nauvoo Seventies Library, and the Nauvoo Agricultural and Manufacturing Association. The sale of stock certificates was the only way to finance such large projects.

Nauvoo City Scrip.
Cities commonly issued scrip to stimulate growth. The Nauvoo scrip was in one denomination of one dollar. Such scrip was usually accepted only in the immediate area. The Saints used many other scrips, including Nauvoo Legion Scrip. This scrip was probably used for the men and for supplies to the legion. The notes were unifaced in the single denomination of one dollar. Arsenal scrip was also issued, which was used to pay for specific equipment such as weapons and ammunition.

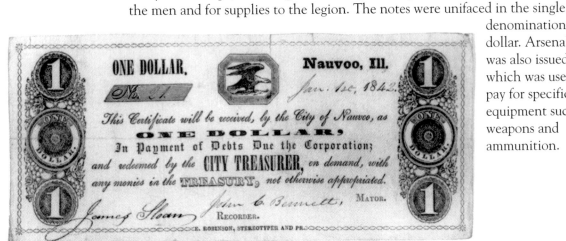

TRANSPORTATION

AS EARLY AS 1831, the Lord told Joseph Smith, "Send forth the elders of my church unto the nations which are afar off; unto the islands of the sea; send forth unto foreign lands; call upon all nations" (D&C 133:8).

The farther west a person traveled, the more difficult travel became—the roads became trails, and trails became virgin prairies or wooded land. The Saints, like others of the period, traveled by boat as much as possible. Travel on land was long and tiring and sometimes next to impossible. The first Church migration from New York to Ohio was accomplished mainly on the Erie Canal from Palmyra to Rochester, New York. Mormon emigrants, missionaries, and Church leaders traveled throughout the United States and Canada during the first few years by whatever method was available to them—dugout canoes on the Missouri River and keelboat and steamboats on the Mississippi River and on other major waterways. Samuel Smith, the first missionary, walked.

Horses and oxen were essential for many Saints traveling to Missouri, Illinois, and on to Winter Quarters. During the winter, sleighs were used, and, eventually, in the East, trains were available. Coastline sailing ships helped missionaries and members to travel along the eastern seashore. Large oceangoing ships took the missionaries to the British Isles and later brought thousands of converts to Nauvoo in the 1840s.

One of the most interesting revelations in the Doctrine and Covenants is section 61. There the Lord discusses the dangers of travel, but ultimately said, "It mattereth not unto me, after a little, if it so be that they fill their mission, whether they go by water or by land" (D&C 61:22).

Ohio-Erie Canal. Some of the water routes used by the Saints included Lake Erie, the Ohio River, the Mississippi River, and canals. A canal-building program eventually connected the Hudson River with the Mississippi River. Law restricted canal barges from traveling more than four miles an hour or ninety-four miles a day. The cabins on the barges were usually divided into male and female quarters, with bunk beds sometimes four high.

Horse Saddle. Horseback was probably the most common and dependable mode of transportation besides foot. Horseback was also one of the fastest means of travel on land. Carriages, coaches, and wagons were also very popular. The roads were in very poor condition. Even the National Road, one of the best in the country, had stumps in the road. With no surfacing on the roads, traveling by wheeled vehicles was difficult, if not impossible, in bad weather.

Nineteenth-Century Sleigh. Travel in the winter was enhanced by a sleigh or sled. Sleighs or sleds were less expensive and easier to construct than wheeled vehicles and were thus affordable to more people.

LIST OF PROVISIONS

FURNISHED BY

REUBEN HEDLOCK,

(Licensed Passenger Broker),

FOR EACH ADULT PASSENGER

FROM

LIVERPOOL TO NEW ORLEANS.

Nineteenth-Century Ship's Bell. The rhythms of daily ship life were regulated by the ship's bell. While the Saints acted in concert, organizing study groups and prayer meetings and cooking together, the tone of the bell nonetheless reminded them of the many monotonous hours crossing the ocean.

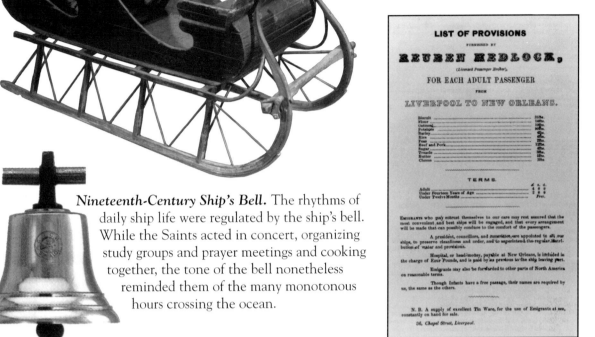

List of Provisions Handbill. This broadside lists the provisions supplied to those emigrating to the United States aboard the Mormon charters. It states fare prices and was issued in 1844 by British Mission president Reuben Hedlock.

The Ship Britannia. This ship carried the first forty Saints from Liverpool, England, to New York City in 1840. A great many Church leaders, missionaries, and migrating Saints traveled in ships along the Atlantic coast and from Europe to the United States. While at sea, they shared the common hazards and discomforts of crossing the ocean with other travelers. These included lack of privacy, inadequate sanitation, disease, storms, poor or inadequate food and water, and the typical harassment and abuse from lustful crew members.

Hardtack (Sea Biscuit). This extremely hard biscuit would not spoil and was a major staple for most passengers and crew members.

Mississippi River Steamboat. A great number of early Saints and settlers traveled by steamboat. Steamboats were also the major transporter of goods, especially along the Mississippi River and other large rivers and lakes. Some steamboats could carry over two hundred tons of merchandise. Steamboats docked in Nauvoo several times a day.

1838 Baltimore and Ohio's No. 16 Locomotive. In July 1836, Joseph and several Church leaders traveled from Utica, New York, to Albany on one of the early railway systems. Missionaries, Church leaders, and converts used the emerging railway system for travel when available or within their budgets.

FRONTIER LIFE AND AMUSEMENTS

THE SAINTS' STRONG community life of service provided them with the necessary spiritual, social, physical, and intellectual foundation for success on the frontier (see D&C 82:19). Frontier life was often difficult for the Saints—especially with the added burden of constant persecution. The majority of the Saints were farmers, a hard way of life for the entire family. Self-sufficiency was the general rule for a frontier family. The community life the Saints established was in contrast to that emphasis on individual independence. Despite the taxing demands of frontier life, the Saints participated in numerous amusements. These amusements were an important part of the social fabric and included hunting, fishing, horseback riding, outdoor games, picnics, circuses, bees, parties, Church activities, and parlor games.

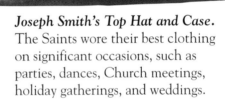

Musket Bullet. Hunting provided food for the Saints, and, when it was done with a friend or in a group, it became recreational. Shooting contests, including turkey shoots, were also held.

Joseph Smith's Top Hat and Case. The Saints wore their best clothing on significant occasions, such as parties, dances, Church meetings, holiday gatherings, and weddings.

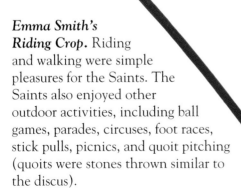

Emma Smith's Riding Crop. Riding and walking were simple pleasures for the Saints. The Saints also enjoyed other outdoor activities, including ball games, parades, circuses, foot races, stick pulls, picnics, and quoit pitching (quoits were stones thrown similar to the discus).

MASONIC HALL

Nauvoo, April 24th 1844, will be presented a

GRAND MORAL ENTERTAINMENT,

To aid in the discharge of a debt, against President Joseph Smith, contracted through the odious persecution of Missouri, and vexatious law suits. His friends and the public will respond to so laudable a call, in patronising the exertions of those who promise rational amusement with usefulness.

The Historical play, a tragedy in five acts, entitled

PIZARRO,
OR
The Death of Rolla.

Peruvians:

Ataliba, King of Quito, - - Mr. J. Hatch.
Rolla and - - - " Lyne.
Alonzo, Commanders of his army - " E. Snow.
An Old Blind Man - - - " G. A. Smith
Ozano - - - - " Howard
Orozembo, (an old cacique) - " J. Greenhow
High Priest - - - " B. Young
A Boy - - - - Master Wooley
Cora, Alonzo's wife - - Miss Goodnell
Servants, Priests, Virgins, Peruvians, Attendants, &c.; by a number of Ladies and Gentlemen who have volunteered for the occasion.

Spaniards.

Pizarro - - - Mr. G. J. Adams.
Almagro - - - " Ward
Gonzalo - - - " Palmer
Davilla, Pizarro's Association - " Porter
Gomez - - - " Kimball
Valverde, Pizarro's Secretary - " Warren
Las Casas, a Spanish Ecclesiastic - " A. Lyman
Sentinel - - - " Nichols
Alvira - - - Mrs. Young

The whole to conclude with the laughable farce of
John Jones, of the War Office.

New scenery, dresses, and decorations, are prepared for the occasion; the whole got up under the direction of Thomas A. Lyne, of the Eastern theatres.

Tickets 50 cents, to be had at the Masonic Hall; of G. J. Adams; or Mr. Scofield. Doors open at 6 o'clock, performance to commence at 7 o'clock. Good music will be in attendance, strict order will be preserved. No money taken at the door. Smoking not allowed. Front seats reserved for the ladies.

Wilford Woodruff's Fishing Pole. Fishing offered settlers an additional food source and could also be very relaxing. The Saints commonly went swimming or went riding on a boat or a steamboat.

Playbill from Nauvoo. In the Mormon community, numerous theatrical presentations were presented at the Masonic Hall or the Cultural Hall. Eliza R. Snow, Brigham Young, and Heber C. Kimball also took part in productions such as *Pizarro*.

Children's Toy Bear from Nauvoo. Young children played with a variety of toys, including kites, dolls, slings, and whistles. They also played many games, such as hoop games, skip rope, hop scotch, marbles, blindman's buff, fox and hounds, and baseball. Ice skating was a favorite activity during the winter.

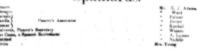

Dominoes Used in Nauvoo. The evening hours in any frontier settlement, particularly during the long winters, were spent in many family activities. Adults enjoyed numerous parlor games, including dominoes.

CLOTHING AND TEXTILES

AN EARLY REVELATION stated, "Let all thy garments be plain" and let "their beauty . . . [be] the work of thine own hands" (D&C 42:40). An important goal for many individuals and families during the first half of the nineteenth century was self-sufficiency. Even when a community such as Nauvoo had several general stores, people could not always get the clothes they wanted or needed. When the Saints left their homes in the East or in the British Isles, most of them were aware of the rugged living conditions on the American frontier and therefore often brought a set of fine clothes with them.

Most of the fabric available in the frontier towns was homespun. Wool and linen were the main sources of home-manufactured clothing. Sheep provided the wool, and flax provided the resource from which linen was made. The women of the family spent a significant amount of time preparing these two items so clothes could be made. Wool was "greased" and then carded with a brushlike instrument. The carder removed the tangles from the wool. The carded wool was spun into yarn on a spinning wheel. The yarn was then woven into fabric on a loom. A woman either took all of these steps herself or bought bulk fabric to fashion into clothing for herself and family. Rugs were braided out of shredded pieces of old rags, and quilts were made from small pieces of material sewn together.

Flax seeds were separated on a rakelike instrument. The stems were then softened and pounded on a brake. Next, the soft inner fibers were spun. Once separated from the outer shells and then combed, they were ready to be spun and woven into linen.

Scissors and Thimble from Nauvoo. After the wool was spun, dyed, woven, and pulled, it was ready to be used to produce dresses, pants, aprons, or shirts. The fabric was cut and sewn using scissors, thimble, and thread.

Emma Smith's Spinning Wheel. The spinning wheel was an essential part of any household because the spinning wheel allowed the Saints to produce their own textiles and clothes. The sheep were washed and sheared. The wool was then sorted and carded, or untangled, so that all fibers were going in one direction. The wool was spun, dyed, and then woven on a loom. The fabric was then pulled (pulled, pushed, and twisted) to make the material shorter, thicker, and stronger.

Buttons Used in Nauvoo. Buttons for clothes were made of bones, shells, tin, or brass.

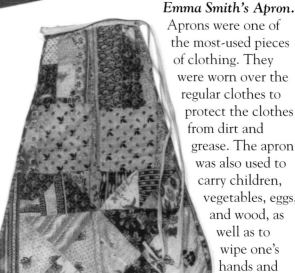

Lucy Mack Smith's Silk Bonnet. Textiles had numerous uses, including the making of bonnets, rugs, quilts, tablecloths, pillows, and samplers.

Hyrum Smith's Wool Pants. Women were primarily responsible for making and mending clothing. These trousers were typical of the period. Hyrum wore these pants during his incarceration in Carthage Jail.

William Marks's Wool and Linen Vest. Besides wool, cotton and linen were two additional sources for making clothes. Cotton was available at the general store but was not a popular material for making everyday clothes. Cotton easily caught fire, and sparks from the fireplace always went astray. Linen was made much like wool and was spun, dyed, and woven, but the material came from a plant called flax. Flax made a finer thread than wool and thus was spun on small spinning wheels.

Iron from Nauvoo. The Saints usually had two sets of clothing—one set for everyday wear and usually made of wool, and a Sunday or "best dress" set, usually made of linen, silk, or bright-colored cotton.

Emma Smith's Apron. Aprons were one of the most-used pieces of clothing. They were worn over the regular clothes to protect the clothes from dirt and grease. The apron was also used to carry children, vegetables, eggs, and wood, as well as to wipe one's hands and brow and to dust furniture.

COMMUNICATION AND NEWS

In 1831, JOSEPH SMITH recorded the following words given to him by inspiration: "Hearken ye people from afar; and ye that are upon the islands of the sea. . . . For verily the voice of the Lord is unto all men; . . . there is no eye that shall not see, neither ear that shall not hear. . . . And the voice of warning shall be unto all people." (D&C 1:1–4.)

Communication and news regarding the Church were important aspects of the Restoration. Letters to family members, friends, and government leaders were an important means of communicating the history and doctrine of the Church. Church newspapers (*The Evening and the Morning Star, Elders' Journal, Messenger and Advocate, Millennial Star, Times and Seasons,* and *Nauvoo Neighbor*) were all crucial vehicles to refute false accusations, correct misunderstandings, and notify members of important Church business. Above all, letters were a vehicle to explain Church history and doctrine to a vast audience.

Times and Seasons *Newspaper.* One of the major means of communication was through the newspapers. They reported important events, advertised services, and announced personal items such as marriages and deaths.

Webb Post Office Box Drawer from Nauvoo. Inside the general store or post office, families had their post boxes, drawers, or slots. Stamps were not used—the postmaster weighed the communication and then wrote the amount due on the outside of the sheets. The sender either paid the postage or allowed the recipient to do so. If postage was due and if the recipient did not pay, the letter remained at the post office, and the postal service took the loss. During the Nauvoo period, the postage rate was five cents for mail within thirty miles. The rate increased with distance.

Letter from Joseph Smith to Emma Smith (13 October 1832). Envelopes were not used. Instead, letters were folded and then sealed with wax. To save postage, some writers wrote horizontally and then vertically over the prior lines. The reader then had to decipher the message. Mail delivery varied from town to town from once a week to daily.

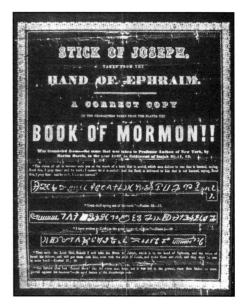

Book of Mormon Broadside (Broadsheet). A broadside was a miniature poster or flyer that was printed on one or both sides. It was used to announce a particular event.

Far West Postmark. A developing postal system allowed Saints to communicate with one another. This postmark, from a letter written by Thomas B. Marsh and sent to Wilford Woodruff, is dated 18 June 1838.

Candle Holders Used in Nauvoo. Communication also took place on a personal level through several ingenious ways. For example, the Saints communicated using candles, lamps, and lanterns. A candle placed in a particular window at night indicated to neighbors that inhabitants were home and ready to entertain guests. Lamps were also used, but lamp oil was much more expensive to burn than candles. Commonly, each family had a tin pierced lantern with its own design. Such a lantern allowed neighbors and friends to recognize a person from some distance because of the lantern's pattern design.

The Newel K. Whitney Store. The general store provided a number of functions for the community. It was a business center, a contact with civilization, and also the general meeting place for the village. People were always gathered inside or outside— talking, arguing, or playing games. Farmers spoke about their crops, merchants sold their services, and women planned social activities.

MISSIONARIES

THE LORD TOLD Joseph Smith, Sr., "If ye have desires to serve God ye are called" (D&C 4:3). Missionaries, along with other priesthood bearers, were told to "take a certificate . . . which shall authorize [them] to perform the duties of [their] calling" (D&C 20:64). Many of the revelations in the Doctrine and Covenants deal with missionary callings. The early missionaries, who often traveled without money, were told, "Whoso receiveth you receiveth me; and the same will feed you, and clothe you, and give you money" (D&C 84:89). As early as 1831, the Lord commanded Church leaders to "send forth the elders of my church unto the nations which are afar off; unto the islands of the sea; send forth unto foreign lands; call upon all nations" (D&C 133:8).

Joseph Smith's Cloak.
The earliest missionaries were commanded to travel without purse or scrip (see D&C 24:18; 84:78, 86). A cloak was necessary when a missionary was traveling without money. Often the cloak provided both a ground cloth and covering if shelter could not be obtained for the night.

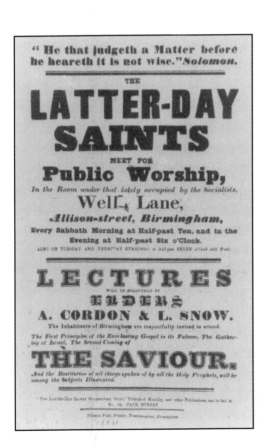

Missionary Handbill. This missionary handbill was used in Birmingham, England, in 1841 by the missionaries to create interest and increase attendance at their meetings. Missionaries preached in homes, businesses, public meeting places, and churches.

TO WHOM IT MAY CONCERN:

This certifies that *John S. Twiss* has been recieved into the church of Jesus Christ of Latter Day Saints, organized on the sixth of April, in the year of our Lord one thousand eight hundred and thirty, and has been ordained a *Elder* according to the rules and regulations of said church; and is duly authorised to preach the gospel, agreeably to the authority of that office.

Given by the direction of a general conference of the authorities of said church, assembled in Nauvoo Ill. on the sixth of April, in the year of our Lord one thousand eight hundred and forty.

James Sloan, Cerk.   *Joseph Smith*, President.

Missionary Certificate. Elders certificates were also used as missionary certificates. A certificate provided authority for the missionary when contact was made with members and nonmembers alike.

David Whitmer's Trunk. Many missionaries traveled with a trunk to carry personal items and missionary publications, especially on long journeys.

Manuscript Copy of Doctrine and Covenants, Section 5. This manuscript was written by Oliver Cowdery. Frequently, after missionaries were called, they made handwritten copies of the Church revelations before going into the mission field. This practice allowed them the opportunity to study and preach from the revelations while on their missions.

W. W. Phelps's Missionary Journal. Journals document the experiences, converts, trials, and joys of missionary life.

FOOD AND MEDICINE

THE SAINTS KNEW that the Lord had given them the bounties of the earth when he stated, "The fulness of the earth is yours" (D&C 59:16). Nevertheless, cooking conditions in the nineteenth century, particularly in the frontier setting, involved a great deal of time, arduous lifting, and reaching. The Lord specifically outlined the use of food and a health code for the Saints in a revelation known as the Word of Wisdom (D&C 89).

Medical practice was still in its infancy during the 1830s and 1840s. The Saints used whatever knowledge was available to them. The Saints also knew that the elders of the Church could "lay their hands" on the sick to heal them (D&C 42:44, 48); they were promised that those "not appointed unto death, shall be healed" (v. 48); and they were instructed that those who were sick should "be nourished with all tenderness, with herbs and mild food" (v. 43).

Plow from Nauvoo. Immediately after arriving at a settlement, the majority of the Saints began farming and raising their own animals. During this time, food was usually scarce, and medicine was nonexistent. After a community was established, food became more plentiful, and some medicine could be obtained. The plow was an essential part of life for the farmer. It allowed him to plant and consequently harvest larger gardens and more productive farms than were otherwise possible.

Hoe Head Used in Nauvoo. After the garden and crops were planted, tools like the hoe further allowed the Saints to harvest large amounts of produce. The Saints took great pride in their gardens and crops, which produced peas, beans, corn, wheat, sweet potatoes, squashes, pumpkins, and melons.

Corn Husker. Among many other tasks, preparing meals included husking corn, gathering and bringing in eggs, making bread (which included preparing the dough, allowing it to rise, and baking the bread), and churning butter. To make butter, the Saints collected fresh milk in a standard pail, poured the milk into several shallow milk pans, and placed the milk in a cool room until the cream came to the top. The cream was then transferred into a churn. After the cream was laboriously churned, the cream turned into butter. The kitchenware had to be very clean because butter absorbs all smells it encounters when it is being made.

FLOUR, meal, pork, lard, butter and cheese, will be received in payment for the Times and Seasons, if delivered.

Times and Seasons Advertisement. This advertisement from the 15 March 1841 edition offers to barter goods in exchange for the paper. When large amounts of food became available, the merchants placed advertisements in the local newspapers to let the people know about the merchants' goods. The availability of extra grocery goods created additional challenges in storage. Food had to be preserved and stored for use throughout the year. Fresh meat could be preserved by drying, smoking, pickling, freezing, or (during the winter months) potting. Vegetables and fruits also needed to be preserved. Vegetables were preserved by pickling them in a brine, which is a mixture of water, vinegar, salt, and spices. The pickling gave the vegetables a strong flavor while preserving them. Fruits were preserved in jams and jellies. A mixture of honey or sugar, fruit, cider, and cinnamon was poured into a crock; a layer of melted mutton fat sealed the crock; and leather or an animal bladder served as a lid.

Earthenware, Including a Plate and Mug Belonging to Joseph and Emma Smith. Some of these ceramics were made in England and were extremely costly.

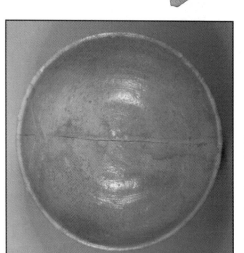

Stoneware Used in Nauvoo. Stoneware was used in everyday life by the Saints in Nauvoo. Stoneware was not as beautiful as china but was much less expensive and more practical. Stoneware was made of special clay that held water without being glazed because the clay contained large amounts of silica. The Saints collected and cleaned the clay, shaped it, and then placed the clay object in a kiln.

Utensils Used by the Saints. The Saints often used trammels, which was a system of hooks that hung on a swinging crane in the fireplace to support pots and kettles over the hearth. Trammels allowed the cook to regulate the amount of heat on the pot. The Saints also cooked with trivets, which were three-legged metal stands that were placed over the fire to support the cooking vessels. The Saints even used toasters. Pots and pans were in short supply because of their expense. The Saints, therefore, usually cooked the whole meal for supper in one pot. In the summer, the heat from the kitchen made the Saints' homes unbearable. To remedy this problem, many of the Saints built summer kitchens, usually apart from the main structure.

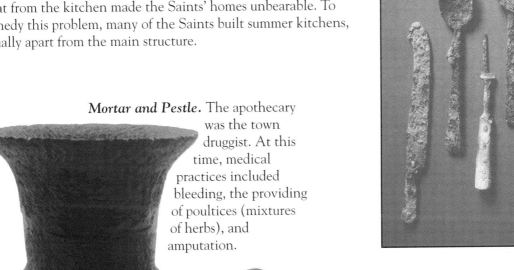

Mortar and Pestle. The apothecary was the town druggist. At this time, medical practices included bleeding, the providing of poultices (mixtures of herbs), and amputation.

Pill Maker. Medicinal herbs were given to the patient in four different ways—as powder, paste, liquid, or a pill. To obtain a pill, the apothecary took the powder, formed it into a paste similar to a dough, and then ran it through a pill maker that formed small balls.

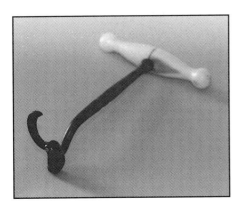

Tooth Puller. A tooth puller was available at the apothecary and was used to pull an aching tooth. The hook was placed into the groove under the tooth's gum, and the tooth was then wedged out.

MILITARY AND WEAPONS

AFTER THE SAINTS were expelled from Jackson County, Missouri, the Lord indicated they should recruit a group of men to help the persecuted Saints in Missouri regain their land. This group became known in Church history as Zion's Camp (see D&C 103:11, 15, 22, 29–40). During a period when local militia units occupied an important aspect of Jacksonian society, the Saints found themselves in need of protection. From this period until the later Utah period, the Saints often found themselves defending their rights through the organization of local militia units. The most famous, the Nauvoo Legion, was chartered by the state of Illinois.

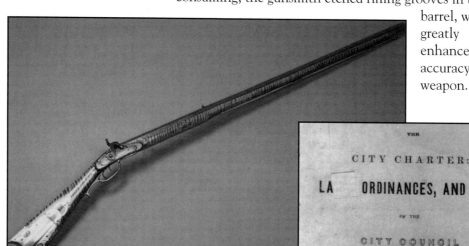

David W. Patten's Horn, Pouch, and Rifle. When persecution arose in Missouri, David W. Patten, a member of the Quorum of the Twelve, led a group of Saints to protect other Saints being harassed by a mob. Patten's group encountered an armed mob, and he was mortally wounded. Gunsmiths were usually blacksmiths who specialized in producing guns. Although the process was time consuming, the gunsmith etched rifling grooves in the gun barrel, which greatly enhanced the accuracy of the weapon.

Nauvoo City Charter, Which Contained the Ordinances of the Nauvoo Legion. Like most frontier communities, Nauvoo received the authority to establish a militia as part of its city charter. The Nauvoo Legion was patterned after a Roman army legion. A legion consisted of ten thousand soldiers, who were subdivided into cohorts of one thousand soldiers. The Nauvoo Legion was made up of two cohorts, despite its enlistment of over five thousand men. One cohort consisted of soldiers with horses.

THE

CITY CHARTER:

LA   ORDINANCES, AND

OF THE

CITY COUNCIL

OF THE

CITY OF NAUVOO.

AND ALSO, THE ORDINANCES

OF THE

NAUVOO LEGION:

FROM THE COMMENCEMENT OF THE CITY TO THIS DATE.

NAUVOO, ILL.
PUBLISHED BY ORDER OF THE CITY COUNCIL.
JOSEPH SMITH, Printer.
July...1842.

Simple Shot Pistol, Box, Ball, Powder, and Pouch of Newel K. Whitney. Most male Saints owned weapons and served in local militia units. Militia service was required for males between eighteen and forty-five in the United States. However, because of Zion's Camp, dirks (long daggers), knives, swords, pistols, muskets, and powder horns were in demand in the Kirtland area.

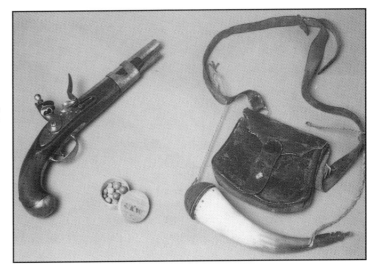

Stiletto and Sheath. The stiletto and sheath was another weapon used by numerous members of the legion.

Sow Cannon Used by the Nauvoo Legion. This sow cannon was manufactured for use in the War of 1812. The Nauvoo Legion was reported to have had five cannons. They were probably stored in the legion arsenal. The cannons were part of an artillery company that was attached to both cohorts. The legion also included a band.

Joseph Smith's Nauvoo Uniform Epaulet and Sash. Americans in all periods have enjoyed participating in and watching military parades. These parades were held often in Nauvoo. The officers wore uniforms, but the average soldier usually wore a badge, scarf, or bright-colored shirt.

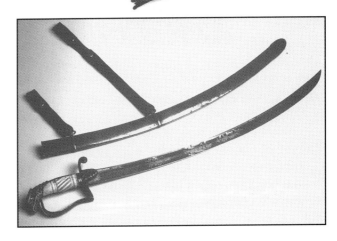

Nauvoo Legion Sword and Scabbard. Officers of the Nauvoo Legion wore these weapons.

LAMANITES

IN AN EARLY revelation dated July 1828, the Lord informed the young prophet that the modern witness of Christ, the Book of Mormon, "shall come to the knowledge of the Lamanites and the Lemuelites, and the Ishmaelites" (D&C 3:18). Joseph was already aware of the Lamanites' (native American Indians) prophetic destiny as a result of his efforts to translate the Book of Mormon.

Shortly after the Church was founded in 1830, several individuals, including Oliver Cowdery, were called to begin the first mission to the Lamanites (see D&C 28:8; 30:6; 32:2). From this early period, and throughout the Prophet's lifetime, contacts with various native American Indian tribes and groups were frequent. Joseph Smith and other Church missionaries and leaders came in contact with Delaware, Potawatomi, Sac, Fox, and Seneca Indian tribes. As the Saints made their way toward the Great Basin in 1846–47, other groups of native American Indians became acquainted with the Saints.

Lithograph by John McGahey of Joseph Smith Preaching to the Indians. John McGahey exhibited this lithograph, which indicated, "Joseph Smith, President of the Church of Jesus Christ of Latter Day Saints addressing the chiefs and braves of several tribes of Indians in the City of Nauvoo, Illinois, North America, June 1843." Joseph Smith considered the Indian tribes of New York, Ohio, Missouri, and throughout the United States as direct descendants of the Lamanites mentioned in the Book of Mormon. He made every effort to convert them to the restored gospel.

Covenant of Lamanite Missionaries from the Ravenna, Ohio Star. After the missionaries were called (D&C 28:8; 30:6; 32:2), they signed a covenant before leaving on their missions.

MANCHESTER, Oct. 17, 1830.
I, Oliver, being commanded of the Lord God, to go forth unto the Lamanites, to proclaim glad tidings of great joy unto them, by presenting unto them the fulness of the Gospel, of the only begotten son of God; and also, to rear up a pillar as a witness where the Temple of God shall be built, in the glorious New-Jerusalem; and having certain brothers with me, who are called of God to assist me, whose names are Parley, Peter and Ziba, do therefore most solemnly covenant before God, that I will walk humbly before him, and do this business, and this glorious work according as he shall direct me by the Holy Ghost; ever praying for mine and their prosperity, and deliverance from bonds, and from imprisonments, and whatsoever may befal us, with all patience and faith.—Amen.   OLIVER COWDERY.
We, the undersigned, being called and commanded of the Lord God, to accompany our Brother Oliver Cowdery, to go to the Lamanites, and to assist in the above mentioned glorious work and business. We do, therefore, most solemnly covenant before God, that we will assist him faithfully in this thing, by giving heed unto all his words and advice, which is, or shall be given him by the spirit of truth, ever praying with all prayer and supplication, for our and his prosperity, and our deliverance from bonds, and imprisonments, and whatsoever may come upon us, with all patience and faith.—Amen.
Signed in presence of
JOSEPH SMITH, Jun.
DAVID WHITMER,
P. P. PRATT,
ZIBA PETERSON,
PETER WHITMER

Iroquois Moccasins. These Iroquois moccasins are made from buckskin, porcupine quills, and glass beads. Fine and decorative items were often worn by young Indians. Dress played an important role in the courting between the sexes. After an Indian couple was married, dress was apparently much less important.

Potawatomi Headdress. Headdresses were worn on formal or religious occasions. They not only symbolized wealth but also vitality that reflected spiritual blessings.

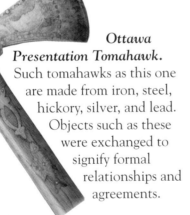

Ottawa Presentation Tomahawk. Such tomahawks as this one are made from iron, steel, hickory, silver, and lead. Objects such as these were exchanged to signify formal relationships and agreements.

Knife and Sheath. This tool could be used for hunting and as a weapon against enemies.

Potawatomi Garter.
The Potawatomi Indians' embroidery of garters, sashes, and shoulder bags incorporated a lot of bead work. These garters had a number of complex patterns. This garter was red and white. White symbolized the powers of peace and purity; red often symbolized conflict or destruction.

COURTS AND JAILS

Two JAILS DOMINATE the landscape of the Doctrine and Covenants—Liberty Jail and Carthage Jail. As a result of confrontations between the Mormons and other residents of Daviess and Caldwell counties in Missouri, Joseph Smith was arrested on the false charge of treason. Since neither Daviess nor Caldwell county had a jail, the Mormon leaders were sent to Liberty, Clay County, Missouri, where they remained from 1 December 1838 to 6 April 1839 in a "lonesome, dark, dirty prison." Between 20 and 25 March 1839, Joseph wrote two letters concerning his experience within these prison walls. Extracts of these letters were eventually included in the Doctrine and Covenants as sections 121, 122, and 123.

The Carthage Jail. Section 135 relates the events of 27 June 1844. The account of the Martyrdom was written by John Taylor, who was imprisoned with Joseph Smith, Hyrum Smith, and Willard Richards and who was an eyewitness to the murders of Joseph and Hyrum.

Handcuffs from Nauvoo. Prisoners who were considered dangerous were placed in handcuffs such as these.

Liberty Jail Window Bars. The jail window measured one foot by two feet and was typical of the period.

Liberty Jail Door. The Liberty Jail is approximately fourteen feet square. The interior consisted of an upper and a lower room. The lower room was the "dungeon" and was accessible only through a trapdoor. Joseph described the entrance to the jail as "a screeching iron door."

Circuit Court Order. Pictured is the Daviess County circuit court order regarding the State of Missouri vs. Joseph Smith, Jr., et al. Joseph and others were brought before Judge King in November 1838 and were charged with several crimes and subsequently jailed in Liberty Jail.

Joseph Smith's Letter from Liberty Jail. Joseph wrote this letter between 20–25 March 1839 to his family and to Church leaders living in Quincy, Illinois. The letter's inspired content became the basis for Doctrine and Covenants sections 121 through 123.

Liberty Jail Stone Floor. Conditions in the jail were difficult, especially for Joseph Smith and his party because of their number. The jail was dark, damp, and cramped; dirty straw was the prisoners' only bedding.

The Liberty Jail. Severe conflicts broke out in 1838 between the Saints and the anti-Mormons. Joseph Smith was blamed for these confrontations, and he and other Church authorities were imprisoned in the Liberty Jail during the winter of 1838–39.

WRITINGS, RECORDS, AND BOOKS

THE EARLY SAINTS kept records in response to a direct commandment. The very day the Church was founded, 6 April 1830, the Prophet Joseph Smith received a revelation in which the commandment was given, "Behold, there shall be a record kept among you" (D&C 21:1). Later, the Lord told the Saints to "become acquainted with all good books" (D&C 90:15). The Lord also advised that "all the names of the whole church . . . be kept in a book" (D&C 20:82).

The doctrines and commandments—Joseph's revelations—were recorded and published in book form. Many ordinances, such as baptisms, confirmations, ordinations to priesthood offices, patriarchal blessings, and temple blessings were also recorded in important Church record books. Another revelation instructs, "Seek ye out of the best books words of wisdom" (D&C 88:118). Many of the sections now found in the Doctrine and Covenants were originally letters, diary entries, minutes of meetings, and prayers. The Saints were told to keep records that would "be put in the archives of [the] holy temple, to be held in remembrance from generation to generation" (D&C 127:9).

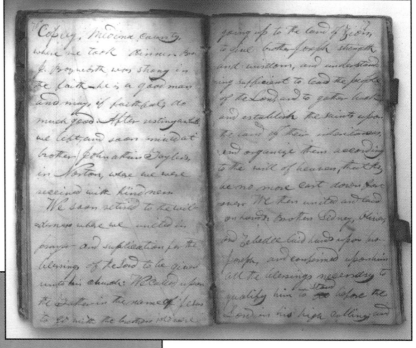

Joseph Smith's Diary—1832–1834. The Lord commanded the Saints to keep a family record. Diaries and journals of Saints are exceptional sources of religious, social, and economic history for descendants and Church members.

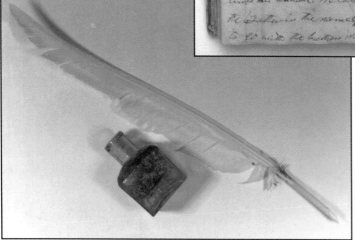

Quill and Ink. Although pencils were available, the most common writing instruments were the quill and ink. Paper was readily obtainable but was very expensive and was, therefore, used conservatively. Goose and turkey quills were most ideal for writing. Ink was made from a wide variety of sources, including gum arabic, sumac, certain berries, and vinegar.

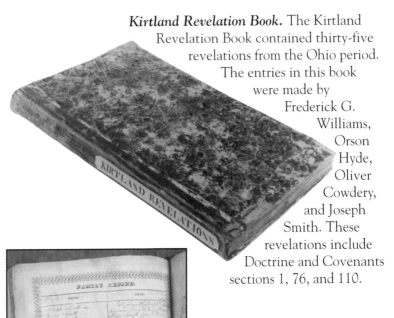

Kirtland Revelation Book. The Kirtland Revelation Book contained thirty-five revelations from the Ohio period. The entries in this book were made by Frederick G. Williams, Orson Hyde, Oliver Cowdery, and Joseph Smith. These revelations include Doctrine and Covenants sections 1, 76, and 110.

Nauvoo House Cornerstone. Cornerstones of the time were often used to deposit precious objects and writings. The Prophet Joseph Smith deposited the original manuscript of the Book of Mormon in the Nauvoo House cornerstone in 1841.

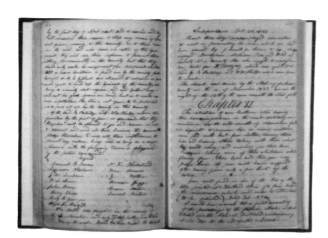

Smith Family Bible. For many families and individuals, a large family Bible was used to record the names, births, baptisms, marriages, and deaths of relatives. The family Bible was an important record book for nineteenth-century Americans.

Relief Society Minute Book. The Relief Society kept a minute book of notes concerning meetings, as did several priesthood quorums in the Church. This Relief Society minute book, as well as the Kirtland Elders' Quorum Record and the Far West Record, provides examples of the variety of information recorded in these important books.

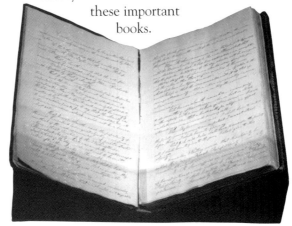

John Whitmer's History. This history of the Church, kept by John Whitmer, was the result of a revelation in D&C 69:2–4. John Whitmer is also considered the first Church historian.

MERCANTILE

As in any frontier town, the Saints' community seemed to revolve around the general store. It was here that the post office was usually located, and thus here news departed and was received, business deals were made, government functions took place, and goods were bartered.

In the Mormon communities, the general store also had religious significance. Newel K. Whitney, who owned the general store in Kirtland, was instructed by the Lord to retain the store (D&C 63:42) and was later called to be a bishop and to keep the Lord's storehouse (D&C 72:9–10). Joseph Smith with his family boarded at the store. Whitney also had a store in Independence. At Joseph Smith's Red Brick Store in Nauvoo, numerous governmental and religious meetings were held. The inventories from stores in Nauvoo clearly show a trend toward ample and diversified physical possessions.

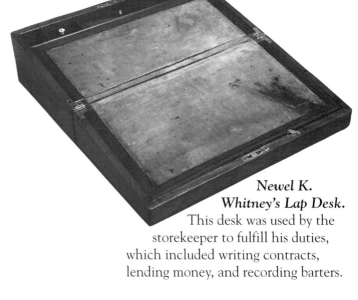

Newel K. Whitney's Lap Desk. This desk was used by the storekeeper to fulfill his duties, which included writing contracts, lending money, and recording barters.

Newel K. Whitney's Store Ledger Book. Two kinds of goods were available for trading at the store—local goods (usually farm products) and "imported" goods (usually goods that could not be produced in the community). Each transaction was recorded in the storekeeper's ledger book.

Joseph Smith's Office Sign from the Red Brick Store. The general store was usually a two-story building that included an office for the storekeeper. Often, the storekeeper was a public official, and the community's business was handled at the store. The front of the store usually had two display windows with a door in the center. One window displayed merchandise for women, and the other window displayed articles for men.

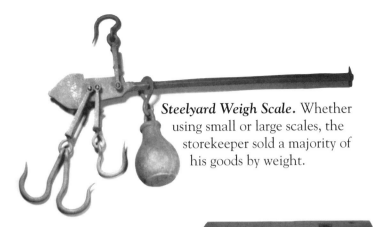

Steelyard Weigh Scale. Whether using small or large scales, the storekeeper sold a majority of his goods by weight.

Nauvoo Blacksmith's Anvil. A farrier worked on horses and wagons, while a blacksmith produced other articles of steel and metal such as kitchen goods (swing cranes) or nails, which were available at the general store.

Glass Pitcher. This pitcher is one of the typical products shipped from the East Coast or from Europe. Steamboats, ships, and canal boats brought a variety of items to Nauvoo and Kirtland for the Saints to consider purchasing. Among these items were beautiful furniture, china, glass, jewelry, medicines, and hardware.

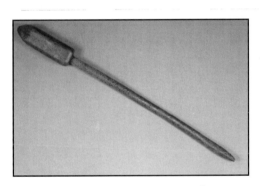

Soldering Iron from Nauvoo. A soldering iron was used by tinsmiths to seal joints that would allow kitchen ware to hold liquid.

Willard Richards's Grooming Kit. Items such as this grooming kit were usually specially ordered from larger cities. Three months or longer were often required for such orders to arrive.

Haun's Mill Face Wheel. This face wheel transferred the force from the waterwheel to the millstones. Milled grains were an indispensable part of the goods sold at the general store.

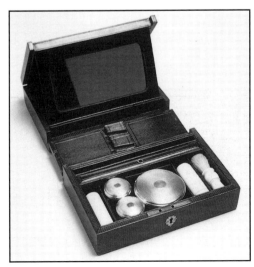

ARCHITECTS, BUILDERS, AND CRAFTSMEN

WHEN THE LORD commanded the Saints to build the Kirtland Temple, he also asked them to build another building. "And again, verily I say unto you, the second lot on the south shall be dedicated unto me for the building of a house unto me, for the work of the printing of the translation of my scriptures, and all things whatsoever I shall command you" (D&C 94:10). Another revelation, dated 19 January 1841, enjoined the Saints to build not only the Nauvoo Temple but also "a house unto my name, . . . and it shall be for a house for boarding, a house that strangers may come from afar to lodge therein" (D&C 124:22–23). This building was known as the Nauvoo House.

The city of Nauvoo was a place where architects, builders, and craftsmen plied their trades in earnest from 1839–46. In addition, stonemasons, carpenters, glazers, cabinetmakers, potters, and inventors arrived in the city to help build it up to the Lord. Some twelve hundred hand-hewn log cabins (the interiors most often whitewashed), three to five frame homes, two or three large brick homes, and many public and business structures were completed during the period.

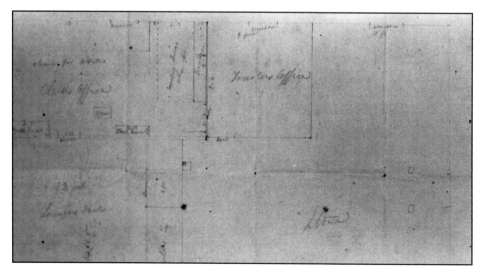

Nauvoo Compass.
A compass was used by architects to draft plans and was also used by most craftsmen. For example, the compass was an important tool for the tinsmith in the production of metal works.

Brick from a Nauvoo Home. Brick builders gathered clay, usually from a riverbank. The clay was mixed with water. The pugmill then produced a paste that was placed in a brick mold. The clay was pressed into the form of a brick, allowed to dry, and then fired in a kiln.

Floor Plans for the Red Brick Store.
Plans were important to construct any home, business, or public building, although in many instances the plans were not detailed.

Plainers, Drill, Auger, and Trowel. Wood, metal, stone, and brick were the major materials used in construction and crafts. The drill and plainer were used to cut and form wood. An auger was also used on wood items, while masons used a trowel in working with mortar and stone.

Wooden Pegs from the Lyman Wight Home in Adam-ondi-Ahman. The first settlers built homes of logs. Later, plank and brick homes became common. Pegs were often used instead of nails to build homes and furniture.

Partial Window Pane from a Nauvoo Home. Until windows became available, the Saints in Kirtland and Nauvoo used paper or cloth instead of glass.

Plaster from a Nauvoo Home. Plaster that was made with lime, sand, and water was a popular exterior finish to many houses and businesses.

DEATH AND BURIAL

DURING THE EARLY period of Church history, an individual was usually born at home and often died at home. For most persons, life's natural rhythms occurred within the family setting. Many people died in their own beds, surrounded by family members who gathered around their loved ones. Burial was completed rapidly—this was before embalming was introduced as a typical burial procedure in America.

For some, however, death and burial occurred in a different setting. Doctrine and Covenants section 135, the official announcement of the martyrdom of Joseph and Hyrum Smith, was included in the modern scriptures just a few months after the tragic events of June 1844.

The Nauvoo Expositor. William and Wilson Law started a dissident newspaper in Nauvoo. Joseph Smith, as mayor, ruled the newspaper a nuisance and ordered it destroyed. This order led to the arrest and confinement of Joseph Smith in Carthage.

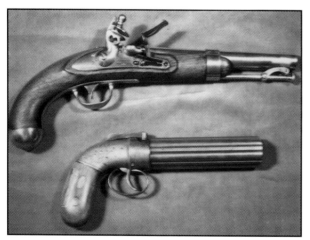

Joseph Smith's and Hyrum Smith's Pistols. When the mob stormed Carthage Jail, Joseph was carrying the pepperbox pistol, and Hyrum was carrying the single-barrel pistol. Joseph and Hyrum used these weapons in an effort to fight off the mob.

Alvin Smith's Tombstone. Family and friends were responsible for buying the coffin and then dressing the body and arranging the funeral. A sexton was the individual who maintained the cemetery and kept proper records. The sexton might also have been a stonecutter who produced tombstones. Alvin Smith, the second son of Joseph and Lucy Mack Smith, was buried in Palmyra, New York.

Stephen Markham's Cane. This cane was used by John Taylor as he tried to fend off the muskets from being thrust through the prisoners' cell door.

The Carthage Jail Door. The Carthage Jail was typical of the period. The jailer's residence was downstairs, and the upstairs contained the cells. The mob fired and fought its way through this door to murder Joseph and Hyrum.

John Taylor's Watch. This watch stopped a bullet from entering John Taylor's chest.

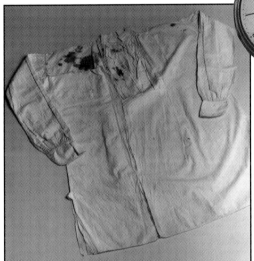

Hyrum Smith's Blood-Stained Shirt. Hyrum was killed almost immediately when a musket ball hit him in the face.

Mob Member's Powder Horn. The powder horn is inscribed "Warsaw regulators, the end of the Polygamist Joseph Smith kilt at Carthage, June 27, 1844."

Hyrum Smith's and Joseph Smith's Death Masks. These original plaster impressions were taken by the Saints immediately after Joseph's and Hyrum's deaths to preserve a likeness of their physical appearance.

1844 Martyrdom Sampler. Mary Ann Broomhead made this sampler at the age of thirteen. She embroidered the verse with her hair.

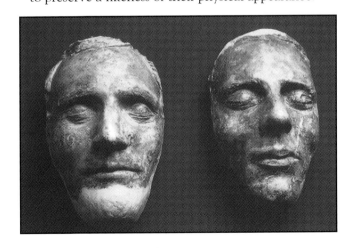

PHOTOGRAPHY AND ART

BEFORE PHOTOGRAPHY WAS invented in 1839 and became accessible to the Saints in Nauvoo in 1844, the Saints relied on sketches, illustrations, and paintings to record events or likenesses of individuals. The sketches were more available and were less expensive than engraved plates for illustrations or a painting. Paintings were usually done with watercolors or oils. Several examples of each medium have survived.

Daguerreotype (Copy) of the City of Nauvoo by Lucian Foster. Photography was invented in 1839 in the form of the daguerreotype. This unique medium allowed the preservation of the past through pictures. The first recorded photographs in Mormon history were taken by Lucian Foster in Nauvoo, Illinois. Foster arrived in Nauvoo on 27 April 1844. By 10 August 1844, he had established a photo studio and was taking landscape and portrait shots.

1842 American Photographic Camera. This wooden daguerreotype camera provided single exposures, approximately three by three inches. The first daguerreotype camera was constructed in 1839, and the camera pictured is patterned after the first model. The rear section of the camera can be moved to focus the object. A screw then can be tightened when the object is focused properly. The mirror at the extreme rear is at a 45-degree angle and served to reverse the image vertically, but not laterally. The camera was undoubtedly similar to one used by Lucian Foster in Nauvoo.

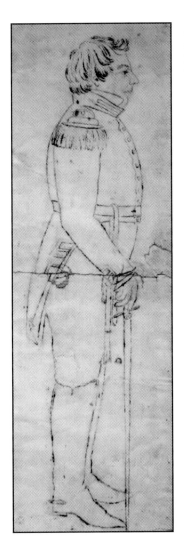

Sketch of the Prophet Joseph Smith. Sketches were often done in preparation for a painting. However, at other times sketches were produced as a less expensive way of recording a person's likeness.

Original Daguerreotype Plate of Eliza R. Snow. Daguerreotypes were popular with the Saints. Although the daguerreotypes were expensive, many Saints obtained their "likenesses" while in Nauvoo. Only a few have been preserved.

Richards Family Silhouettes. Silhouettes were another less expensive form of recording a person's likeness. These two silhouettes were of Willard Richards's parents, Rhoda and Joseph Richards. Church historians believe Rhoda actually designed and cut the silhouettes.

Painting of Joseph Knight, Sr. Joseph Knight was an early disciple of the Church. One of the Church's earliest congregations was established in Colesville, New York, and met at the home of Joseph and Polly Knight. Having a painting made was usually too expensive and time consuming for the average individual.

PIONEERS AND TRAILS

THE NEIGHBORING TOWNS around Nauvoo, Illinois—including their merchants, innkeepers, blacksmiths, saddlers, and the like—had never before seen a mass movement like the one they witnessed in 1846. The City of Joseph was alive with workshops—scattered throughout the city—as the Saints prepared to go west. Within a year, several communities around Winter Quarters, Nebraska, were established as workshops to help the Saints prepare for their migration to the Great Basin.

The pioneers sold their property to raise money for the trip. The appropriate tools and goods had to be loaded into wagons and buggies. The decision concerning which items to take was difficult. Few beloved keepsakes, such as painted china or heavy tables with fine clawed feet, could be included in the load. Usually only the most indispensable items could be taken, and all other objects had to be sacrificed to lighten the load. The proper wagons, animals, and tools were necessary if the Saints were to arrive safely at their destination. Section 136 of the Doctrine and Covenants, entitled "The Word and Will of the Lord," gave the pattern for the organization of the pioneers. The first vanguard company, consisting of 148 people and 72 wagons and carriages—pulled by 211 horses, mules, and oxen—arrived in the Great Basin in July 1847.

Handcart Used by Mormon Pioneers. In 1856, financial stress led Church leaders to bring groups of Saints across the plains using handcarts. The handcarts were pushed or pulled and could carry from one to five hundred pounds.

Brigham Young's Compass. A compass was an important instrument for any traveler on the plains.

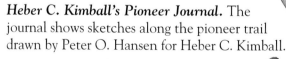

Heber C. Kimball's Pioneer Journal. The journal shows sketches along the pioneer trail drawn by Peter O. Hansen for Heber C. Kimball.

Oxen Yoke. The first group of Saints crossed the plains in wagons. Most often, oxen were used to pull the wagons because oxen had greater endurance, did not need as much water as horses or mules, and could graze easily along the trail.

John Young's Flour Sack. Grain and other pioneer provisions were very important to the Saints leaving Winter Quarters. Many times they bartered clothes, furniture, and crops in return for these pioneer necessities.

Orson Pratt's Telescope and Theodolyte with Box. John Taylor brought back these scientific instruments from England to help the Saints on their trek west. A theodolyte is a surveyor's tool, a necessity for laying out a new city.

Brass Bucket. This bucket belonged to pioneer T. S. Allred. The pioneer journey was extremely arduous. Usually, only provisions that aided the Saints in crossing the plains were included for the journey. Items such as this bucket served many purposes.

Brigham Young's Wagon. This was Brigham Young's wagon when he traveled from Winter Quarters to the Salt Lake Valley.

J. McAllister's Wooden Leg. Great diversity existed among the Saints who crossed the plains. They came from a variety of social, economic, and ethnic backgrounds and had to manage countless and often severe physical and emotional challenges.

Thomas Bullock's Pioneer Company Journal. In his journal, Bullock lists the companies of the Vanguard Pioneer Company—symbolic of twelve men from each of the tribes of Israel.

SECTION THREE

THE DOCTRINE AND COVENANTS IN CHURCH HISTORY

I N 1880, CHARLES WOODWARD, an unremitting antagonist of the Church, offered his personal *Mormon Americana* library for sale. His descriptions of the items in his collection of Mormon and Utah books say much about his attitude toward the Saints. Regarding the Book of Commandments, Woodward asserted, "People who know just enough of Mormonism to call the Book of Mormon the 'Mormon Bible' . . . will read with distrust or indifference, if they read at all, the assertion which I unhesitatingly make, that this book, if valued by its importance, would bring a larger price than was ever paid for a single volume" (*Bibliothica-scallawagiana* [New York, 1880], p. 4; see also Peter Crawley, "Joseph Smith and a *Book of Commandments*," *Princeton University Library Chronicle* 42 [Autumn 1980]: 18).

The Book of Commandments is, of course, the precursor to the first edition of the Doctrine and Covenants (1835). The history of this modern scripture is both colorful and profound. The argument can be made that Woodward was largely correct when he unblushingly declared the Book of Commandments to be "the whole of Mormonism" (*Bibliothica-scallawagiana*, p. 4). The most complete and comprehensive treatment of the development of the Doctrine and Covenants is Robert J. Woodford, "The Historical Development of the Doctrine and Covenants" (Ph.D. diss., Brigham Young University, 1974); the material in this section relies heavily on Woodford's work (see also Robert J. Woodford, "The Story of the Doctrine and Covenants," *Ensign* 14 [December 1984]: 32–39; Robert J. Woodford, "How the Revelations in the Doctrine and Covenants Were Received and Compiled," *Ensign* 15 [January 1985]: 27–33; and Melvin J. Petersen, "Preparing Early Revelations for Publication," *Ensign* 15 [February 1985]: 14–20).

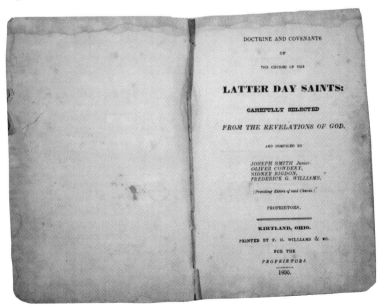

1835 Doctrine and Covenants.

*David White Rogers's Painting of Joseph Smith
(ca. 1842).*

THE DEVELOPMENT OF THE DOCTRINE AND COVENANTS

THE STORY OF the Doctrine and Covenants begins in Manchester, New York, in 1820 when Joseph Smith prayed for guidance in the woods near his parents' log-cabin home. Joseph's first revelation—now known as the First Vision—occurred when the Father and the Son answered the young boy's prayer.

Several years later, Joseph again sought the Lord in prayer. An angelic personage visited him in the upper room of his parents' home not far from the location of the First Vision. From that time forward, Joseph received countless revelations regarding the work of God.

These revelations contained important information for the disciples who began to gather around the young Prophet. Following the organization of the Church on 6 April 1830, Joseph continued to receive the "mind and will of the Lord." "The Articles and Covenants," now known as sections 20 and 22, were "read by Joseph Smith, Jr. and received by [the] unanimous voice of the whole congregation" at the first Church conference, held in Fayette, New York, on 9 June 1830 (Far West Record, 9 June 1830, Archives Division, Church Historical Department, The Church of Jesus Christ of Latter-day Saints, Salt Lake City, Utah, hereafter cited as LDS Church Archives; a published source is Donald Q. Cannon and Lyndon W. Cook, eds., *Far West Record* [Salt Lake City: Deseret Book Co., 1983], p. 1). At the second conference of the Church, in September 1830, the Saints voted to receive from Joseph "Revelations and Commandments for this Church" (Far West Record, 26 September 1830; see Cannon and Cook, *Far West Record*, p. 3).

These revelations, recorded in manuscript form, were invaluable to the Church. They offered instructions regarding many aspects of Church government and addressed specific duties of individual members who asked Joseph for guidance. At the conference during which the Doctrine and Covenants was approved for publication, the Prophet Joseph Smith said these modern revelations were the "foundation of the Church and the salvation of the world" (Far West Record, 12 November 1831; see Cannon and Cook, *Far West Record*, p. 32).

Although all of the Prophet's revelations were certainly important, especially for those to whom they were given, not all of them are included in the Doctrine and Covenants. Several were published in official Church newspapers and later in the *History of the Church*. Many more remain in manuscript form in the Archives Division of the Church Historical Department, in the Library-Archives of the Reorganized Church of Jesus Christ of Latter Day Saints, in the Special Collections Department of the Harold B. Lee Library at Brigham Young University, and in several private collections.

Many of the early revelations were marked by the distinction of having a specific name attached to them, by which they were known to the Saints. They include "The Lord's Preface" (D&C 1); "Articles and Covenants of the Church" (D&C 20 and 22); "The Law of the Church" (D&C 42); "The Vision" (D&C 76); "The Prophecy on War" (D&C 87); "The Olive Leaf" (D&C 88); "The Word of Wisdom" (D&C 89); "Revelation on Priesthood" (D&C 107); and "The Appendix" (D&C 133). The fact that these revelations were distinguished by a name or title indicates their importance and significance to the early Church.

Many revelations were received before the Church was legally organized in 1830. We do not know when the first revelations were written down, but the Lord instructed Joseph in July

1830 to "continue in calling upon God in my name, and writing the things which shall be given thee" (D&C 24:5). Some attempt to organize these recorded revelations was made very early. Joseph Smith noted, "Shortly after we had received the above revelations [sections 24, 25, and 26], Oliver Cowdery returned to Mr. Peter Whitmer's, Sen., and I began to arrange and copy the revelations, which we had received from time to time; in which I was assisted by John Whitmer, who now resided with me" (*History of the Church* 1:104).

After Joseph and his scribes recorded the first revelations, several handwritten manuscript copies were made. Very few original manuscripts have survived. While more than two hundred extant copies of the revelations in the Doctrine and Covenants are preserved in various locations, only a few can actually be identified as original.

As the work of the Restoration spread from where Joseph Smith was living, missionaries carried copies of the revelations to assist them in their work. Members in outlying areas relied on these copies to help them keep abreast of the work. Jared Carter, one among the many missionaries of the period, noted in his journal in 1832, "On Sunday 20th of May, [we] held meeting in this place [Vermont]. We found our brethren in trials in some respect. Brother Gideon and Brother Silvester Smith preached and we preached and read revelations to the congregation and it appeared that the Spirit of God rested upon the congregation." On another occasion, Brother Carter wrote, "[I] went on my way for Kirtland. [I] arrived in Kirtland on the evening of the 19th of October 1832 where I met some of my brethren and heard them read revelations which caused my heart to rejoice." (Jared Carter, Journal, LDS Church Archives.)

Later, Orson Pratt confirmed Carter's statements by writing: "We often had access to the manuscripts when boarding with the Prophet; and it was our delight to read them over and over again, before they were printed. And so highly were they esteemed by us, that we committed some to memory; and a few we copied for the purpose of reference in our absence on missions; and also to read them to the Saints for their edification. These copies are still in our possession." ("Explanation of Substituted Names in the Covenants," *The Seer* 2 [March 1854]: 228.)

One particular revelation, "The Articles and Covenants" of the Church (D&C 20), was considered so important that it was copied on numerous occasions. The Lord specifically identified this revelation as one of the most significant texts for a missionary when he told Joseph Smith, "Behold thus saith the Lord unto you my servants, that I have chosen Lincoln [Haskin] to be a servant unto me. Wherefore verily I say unto you, let him be ordained and receive the Articles and Covenants which I have given unto you and some of the commandments that he may go forth and proclaim my gospel whithersoever I will send him in the congregations of the wicked. And in as much [as he] is faithful, I will prosper him. Even so, Amen." (Kirtland Revelation Book, 27 February 1832, LDS Church Archives.)

Although Joseph's revelations were highly prized, not all of them were recorded, and others were written only in part. Joseph expressed some caution regarding public availability of certain revelations, in order to protect the safety of those mentioned, but most of his revelations were intended for use in the Church. With time, Church leaders saw the importance of making these revelations more accessible to Church members in general. The hand-copied manuscripts being circulated often contained errors of transmission, and these errors contributed to the need to publish a correct version of the revelations.

During the important series of Church conferences held in Hiram, Ohio, between 1 and 11 November 1831, Joseph was asked to "correct those errors or mistakes [caused by careless copying] which he may discover by the Holy Spirit while reviewing the revelations and commandments" (Far West Record, 8 November 1831; see Cannon and Cook, *Far West Record*, p. 29). Church leaders also agreed to print these revelations—more than sixty at this point—in book form under the title "Book of Commandments for the Government of the Church of Christ" in an edition of ten thousand copies. Oliver Cowdery was appointed by the vote of the conference to carry the corrected manuscripts to Missouri for printing.

Earlier, in June 1831, William Wines Phelps, a New York newspaperman, converted to the Church and within a month was called to serve as the first Church printer (see D&C 57:11–12). At a Church conference held in the newly established Church headquarters at Kirtland, Ohio, Phelps was called to travel to Independence, Missouri—an appointed gathering place for the Saints. On the way to Zion, he was directed to purchase a press and type for the Church's first printing operation. Once established in Jackson County, Phelps began publishing a newspaper in support of the Church. Phelps published many revelations for the first time in *The Evening and the Morning Star*, known by many simply as the *Star*.

Joseph's work of correcting and revising manuscripts included those revelations already published in the *Star*, which in some cases had been taken from inaccurate, handwritten copies. As noted, publication in the *Star* represented the earliest attempt to publish Joseph Smith's revelations.

Some opposition to the publication of the revelations in book form arose. David Whitmer objected strenuously to the proposal. He believed the revelations were "not law." He said, "They were given mostly to individuals . . . for their individual instruction, and the Church had no need of them. . . . It was not the will of the Lord that the revelations should be published." (See David Whitmer, *An Address to All Believers in Christ* [Richmond, Mo., 1887], pp. 53–54.)

Despite David Whitmer's personal opposition to the will of the conference, the vote stood. During one of the breaks between meetings, Joseph received what was to become the introductory revelation in the book (see D&C 1). Known as "The Preface," this revelation came as a result of Joseph Smith's request for the Lord's approval to publish the revelations in book form. In it, the Lord not only authorized its publication but also commanded the Saints and all who would listen to "search these commandments, for they are true and faithful, and the prophecies and promises which are in them shall all be fulfilled" (D&C 1:37).

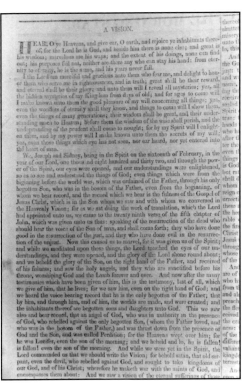

The Evening and the Morning Star. Like many of the important early revelations, Doctrine and Covenants 76 was published in the Church's first newspaper, *The Evening and the Morning Star*. The revelation was entitled simply "A Vision."

On the final day of the conference, a revelation now known as Doctrine and Covenants section 70 was received. The Lord called Joseph Smith, Oliver Cowdery, John Whitmer, Sidney Rigdon, William W. Phelps, and Martin Harris to be "stewards over the revelations and commandments" (D&C 70:1, 3). Eventually, this group became known as the Literary Firm and took the responsibility to publish the revelations.

In January 1832, the majority of the manuscript revelations were hand carried from Kirtland to Missouri by Oliver Cowdery and John Whitmer. In April, Joseph Smith, in company with several others, arrived in the new Mormon settlement with paper for the press.

In several issues of the *Star*, Phelps printed many of Joseph's revelations for the first time. However, almost immediately discrepancies between the printed version and the original revelations were noticed. Oliver Cowdery noted, "On the revelations we merely say, that we were not a little surprised to find the previous print so different from the original. We have given them a careful comparison. . . . Thus saying we cast no reflections upon those who were entrusted with the responsibility of publishing them in Missouri." (*Star*, January 1835 [Kirtland reprint].) Cowdery noted earlier, "It is also proper for us to say, that in the first 14 numbers [of the *Star*], in the Revelations, are many errors, typographical, and others, occasioned by transcribing the manuscript; but as we shall have access to originals, we shall endeavor to make proper corrections" (*Star*, September 1834 [Kirtland reprint]).

As many as twenty-three revelations were originally published in the *Star* during this period. The Church also used other means of publishing the revelations, including the use of "broadsheets," better known as handbills (sections 59, 88, and 89; and on one handbill, sections 101 and 109).

In March 1832, Joseph Smith went to the Lord to ask some specific questions regarding the publication of the commandments and revelations he had received. He asked on that occasion, "First—shall we procure the paper required of our brethren in this letter, and carry it with us or not, and if we do, what monies shall we use for the purpose?" The Lord responded, "It is expedient saith the Lord unto you, that the paper shall be purchased for the printing of the books for the Lord's commandments. And it must needs be that you take it with you, for it is not expedient that my servant Martin should as yet go up unto the land of Zion. Let the purchase be made by the Bishop. If it needs must be by hire, whatsoever is done let it be done in the name of the Lord." (Joseph Smith revelation, 20 March 1832, Newel K. Whitney Collection, Special Collections, Harold B. Lee Library, Brigham Young University, Provo, Utah; hereafter cited as HBLLBYU.)

Unpublished Revelation of Joseph Smith (20 March 1832). This revelation is written in a question-and-answer format and deals with the paper needed for the publication of the commandments and revelations.

During a meeting of the Literary Firm held on 30 April 1832, the number of copies of the Book of Commandments to be printed was decreased to three thousand copies. At this meeting, W. W. Phelps, Oliver Cowdery, and John Whitmer were appointed to supervise the book's actual publication.

By December, the Book of Commandments was ready for printing, although the actual printing took a long time on Phelps's handpress. In February 1833, W. W. Phelps secured a copyright for the book; in June, the printing had proceeded far enough to begin thinking about bindings. On 20 July, as the final pages were being printed, a mob destroyed the Phelps's home and printing office. Five 32-page "signatures" had been struck off—leaving one or two signatures yet to be printed when the armed group entered the printing establishment.

Manuscript Copy of Doctrine and Covenants 64. Section 64 was the last revelation printed for the Book of Commandments. To show where the printing had stopped, Phelps circled the word *Ephraim.* Ironically, the full passage states, "The rebellious are not of the blood of Ephraim" (D&C 64:36).

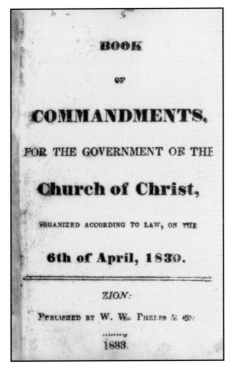

1833 Book of Commandments.

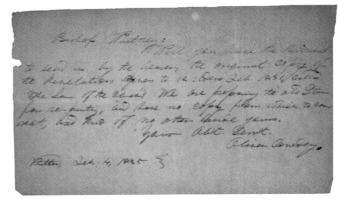

The mob's main purpose was to stop the publication of the *Star,* but most of the paper on which the Book of Commandments was being printed was also lost in the fire and destruction of the printing facility. The press and type were thrown out of the second-story window into the street below.

Through some heroic efforts, rescuers salvaged several galley-proof sheets. These incomplete copies of the Book of Commandments were eventually bound and circulated, and twenty copies are known to have survived. The book itself was often cited officially and used by missionaries.

Within a year of the destruction of the Church's printing establishment in Missouri, Sidney Rigdon and Oliver Cowdery were set apart to publish the revelations in Kirtland, Ohio. Funds were collected for the printing. Oliver Cowdery began to review the original manuscripts and to prepare them for publication in a reprint of the *Star.* On 4 February 1835, Oliver wrote Bishop Newel K. Whitney for the "original copy of the revelation given to 12 elders on February 1831 called 'The Law of the Church' [see D&C 42]" (Newel K. Whitney Collection, Special Collections, HBLLBYU).

During this process of revision and publication, another source was used in preparing the revelations for printing— namely, the Kirtland Revelation Book. This book contained thirty-five Ohio revelations recorded by several different individuals. Within a short time, the new publication was ready for binding in Cleveland under the title, Doctrine and Covenants of the Church of the Latter Day Saints, published in Kirtland, Ohio,

Letter from Oliver Cowdery to Bishop Whitney (4 February 1835). This letter from Cowdery asks Bishop Whitney for the copy of "The Law of the Church" so that it could be printed correctly.

in 1835.
1835 Doctrine and Covenants.

The change in title from Book of Commandments to Doctrine and Covenants reflected a change of content. Unlike the earlier book, which contained only revelations or commandments, the Doctrine and Covenants was basically two books in one. The first part contained seven lectures (later known as the Lectures on Faith) which, as the heading of the first lecture indicated, were "On the Doctrine of the Church of the Latter Day Saints"; the second part was entitled, "Covenants and Commandments of the Lord, to His Servants of the Church of the Latter Day Saints." The first American edition, then, published in Kirtland, Ohio, contained the 7 Lectures on Faith, 102 sections, and the proceedings of the 17 August 1835 general assembly.

Broadside of the First Lecture of the Lectures on Faith. This is the first of seven Lectures on Faith. The type used to print this broadside is the same type that was used to print the 1835 Doctrine and Covenants.

Changes in later editions of the manuscripts and in the 1833 Book of Commandments, including the 1835 edition, were grammar and syntax corrections, changes in archaic words, additions of surnames that were often incomplete or omitted entirely in the manuscript and in early printed versions, additions of words to clarify and enlarge upon the principles mentioned in the revelations, the addition of organizational names and offices, and a few deletions.

A second American edition appeared in 1844, a few months after the deaths of Joseph and Hyrum Smith, under the title of The Doctrine and Covenants of the Church of Jesus Christ of Latter Day Saints. This edition contained 111 sections. Two more editions of the Doctrine and Covenants were published in Nauvoo (the 1845 and 1846 editions).

A European edition of the modern scripture was published in England in 1845 (known as the first European edition), based on the second American edition. As the Church expanded in the British Isles and as the Saints continued their settlement in the Rocky Mountains, several European editions of the Doctrine and Covenants were published. (Early non-English editions include Welsh [1851]; Danish [1852]; German [1876]; and Swedish [1888].)

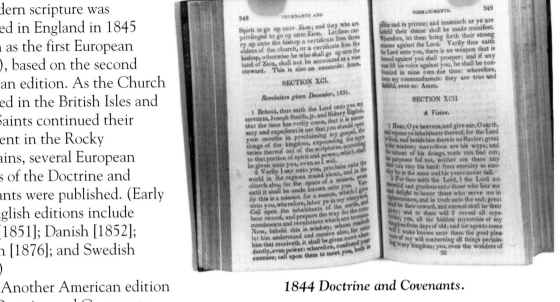

1844 Doctrine and Covenants.

Another American edition of the Doctrine and Covenants was published in Salt Lake City in 1876. This edition was the first one published in the United States after the 1846 Nauvoo edition. The book was divided into verses for the first time, the article on marriage was deleted, and several other revelations, including section 132, were added, for a total of 136 sections. In several revelations (sections 78, 82, 92, 96, 103, 104, and 105), Joseph had purposely added fictitious names of people, places, and things. Orson Pratt replaced these fictitious names, which were used to protect the identities of Church members in earlier versions, with the real names (except in D&C 82:11).

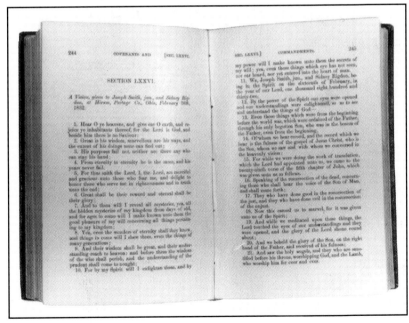

1876 Doctrine and Covenants.

More than thirty printings of the Doctrine and Covenants were made between the 1876 and 1920 editions. Vest-pocket versions, "double" and "triple combinations," and some with a concordance were among those available to the Saints.

In 1908, another edition of the Doctrine and Covenants was published by the Church in Utah. An "Official Declaration," known as the Manifesto, was included, and footnotes that had been added in the 1879 edition were retained.

The 1921 edition of the Doctrine and Covenants deleted the Lectures on Faith but retained the book's title. Double-column pages, an index, longer chapter headings, and revised footnote references were also added to this edition.

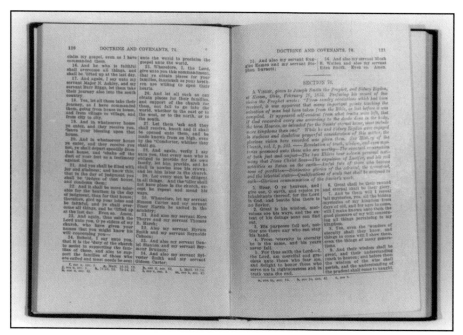

1921 Doctrine and Covenants.

The 1981 edition of the Doctrine and Covenants included, for the first time, Joseph Smith's "Vision of the Celestial Kingdom" as section 137; Joseph F. Smith's "Vision of the Redemption of the Dead" as section 138; and the 1978 First Presidency letter announcing the extension of the priesthood to all worthy males as "Official Declaration—2."

Several of Joseph Smith's revelations remain in manuscript form and are presently unpublished. Many other revelations have been published in the *History of the Church* but have not been canonized as part of the standard works of the Church. (For a list of Joseph Smith's uncanonized revelations, both published and unpublished, see Lyndon W. Cook, *The Revelations of the Prophet Joseph Smith: A Historical and Biographical Commentary of the Doctrine and Covenants* [Salt Lake City: Deseret Book Co., 1985], Appendix B, "Uncanonized Revelations Received by Joseph Smith [1831–44]," pp. 361–64.)

1981 Doctrine and Covenants.

Some of the revelations of the prophets who succeeded Joseph in the Church's Presidency have been published in Church periodicals and books; others remain in manuscript form only. These manuscripts in the Church archives testify that the Lord continues to speak to his servants, the prophets. The published collection of revelations known as the Doctrine and Covenants confirms the Saints' beliefs as outlined in one of the Articles of Faith: "We believe all that God has revealed, all that He does now reveal, and we believe that He will yet reveal many great and important things pertaining to the Kingdom of God" (Articles of Faith 1:9).

COMMANDMENTS IN THE DOCTRINE AND COVENANTS

SEVERAL REVELATIONS COMMANDED the Saints to perform specific tasks—including collecting and publishing certain items (see D&C 123 and 124:2–3). In consequence of the injustices received at the hands of their enemies, Joseph Smith set forth the Saints' duties in relation to their persecutors in March 1839. While languishing in Liberty Jail, Joseph wrote: "And again, we would suggest for your consideration the propriety of all the saints gathering up a knowledge of all the facts, and sufferings and abuses put upon them by the people of this State; and also of all the property and amount of damages which they have sustained, both of character and personal injuries, as well as real property" (D&C 123:1–2).

The members of the Church were also commanded to "gather up" the "libelous histories" found in magazines, encyclopedias, and other works.

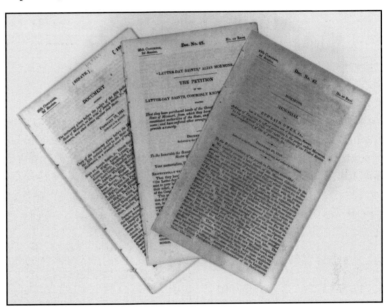

United States Senate and Congressional Documents. The Saints collected letters and affidavits concerning the persecution of the Mormons in northwest Missouri in 1838 and 1839. They sent this information to the federal government, and the government subsequently published this material as government documents.

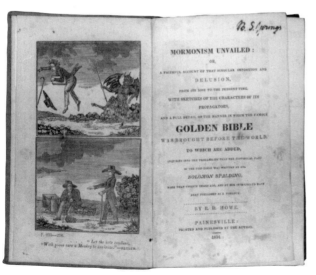

1834 Anti-Mormon Book, Mormonism Unvailed. This book was published by E. D. Howe in Painesville, Ohio. Joseph Smith was once told by the angel Moroni that Joseph's name would be known for good and evil. As a result of Joseph's prophetic ministry, many anti-Mormon articles, pamphlets, and books were published.

When the Saints settled in Nauvoo, Joseph Smith received an important revelation on 19 January 1841. This long revelation (the longest in the Doctrine and Covenants) charged the Prophet to "make a solemn proclamation" to the rulers of all nations (see D&C 124:2–14, 16–17, 107). Not until 1845, following Joseph's assassination, did the Quorum of the Twelve Apostles under the direction of Brigham Young finally fulfill this commandment. Under the date of 6 April 1845, a sixteen-page pamphlet was printed in New York.

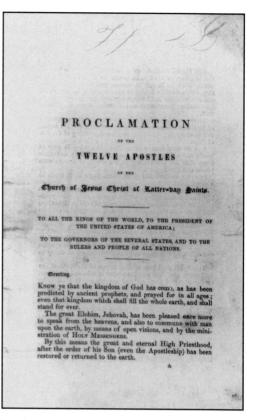

1845 Proclamation. Written by Parley P. Pratt and published in New York, the proclamation was addressed to "all the kings of the world, to the President of the United States of America; to the governors of the several states, and to the rulers and people of all nations."

As the Saints gathered to the Nauvoo area, the Lord directed through Joseph Smith that it was His will that they should "build up a city unto my name upon the land opposite the city of Nauvoo, and let the name of Zarahemla be named upon it. And let all those who . . . have desires to dwell therein, take up their inheritance in the same, as well as in the city of Nashville." (D&C 125:3–4.) Through Isaac Galland, Church members purchased securities Galland offered in an area known as the "half-breed lands." It is estimated that nearly two thousand Saints settled in the area.

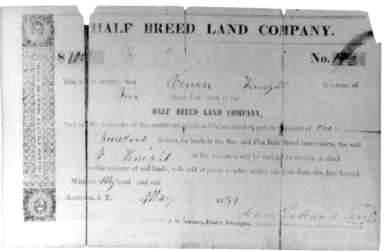

Share Certificate in the Half-Breed Land Company. Five shares of stock were purchased by Vinson Knight for one hundred dollars. Later it was discovered that there was no clear title to the half-breed lands.

THE JOSEPH SMITH TRANSLATION AND THE DOCTRINE AND COVENANTS

FOLLOWING THE PUBLICATION of the Book of Mormon in March 1830 and the establishment of the Church in April, Joseph Smith began to fulfill his various duties as the leader of the Church, including the office of translator (see D&C 21:1). In December 1831, he wrote, "I resumed the translation of the Scriptures, and continued to labor in this branch of my calling with Elder Sidney Rigdon as my scribe" (*History of the Church* 1:238). From this statement, we know that the Prophet obviously considered the efforts to translate the Bible to be part of his prophetic calling.

Joseph Smith's 1828 Bible. Joseph Smith and Oliver Cowdery acquired a copy of the King James Version of the Bible in October 1829 for the price of three dollars and twenty-five cents from the E. B. Grandin Bookstore in Palmyra.

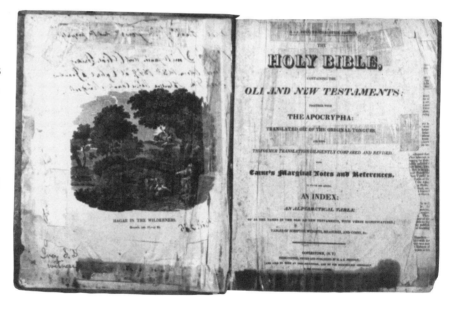

The process of translating the Bible probably began as early as the summer of 1830. The material now located in the Pearl of Great Price known as the "Visions of Moses" contains the Joseph Smith Translation (JST) portion of the first chapters of Genesis. The process of translation continued from June 1830 as Oliver Cowdery and John Whitmer acted as scribes. Eventually they both were called to other duties and Emma, the Prophet's wife, to act as scribe (see D&C 25:6). Later, on 10 December 1830, the Lord spoke to Sidney Rigdon: "And a commandment I give unto thee—that thou shalt write for him; and the scriptures shall be given, even as they are in mine own bosom" (D&C 35:20).

Subsequent to this appointment, Sidney Rigdon became Joseph's principal scribe. Following the reception of the "prophecy of Enoch," Joseph and Sidney were commanded by the Lord, "Behold, I say unto you that it is not expedient in me that ye should translate any more until ye shall go to the Ohio" (D&C 37:1). Following Joseph's and Sidney's arrival in Kirtland, the Lord said, "And again, it is meet that my servant Joseph Smith, Jun., should have a house built, in which to live and translate" (D&C 41:7). Several days later, the Lord admonished Joseph, "Thou shalt ask, and my scriptures shall be given as I have appointed, and they shall be preserved in safety" (D&C 42:56).

Joseph Smith's Marked Bible, Pages 746–47 (Revelation, Chapters 7–10).

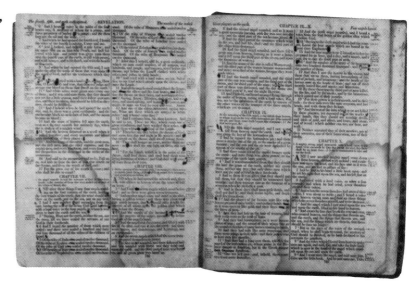

In March 1831, Joseph Smith received the following: "And now, behold, I say unto you, it shall not be given unto you to know any further concerning this chapter, until the New Testament be translated, and in it all these things shall be made known; wherefore I give unto you that ye may now translate it, that ye may be prepared for the things to come" (D&C 45:60–61).

The translation of Matthew 1 commenced on the following day, 8 March 1831. Through a series of interruptions, the Prophet continued his work. In January 1832, a revelation stated, "Now, verily I say unto you my servants, Joseph Smith, Jun., and Sidney Rigdon, saith the Lord, it is expedient to translate again; . . . it is expedient to continue the work of translation until it be finished" (D&C 73:3–4). As is well known, shortly thereafter, while translating the Gospel of John, Joseph and Sidney received an important revelation known then as "The Vision" and now as section 76.

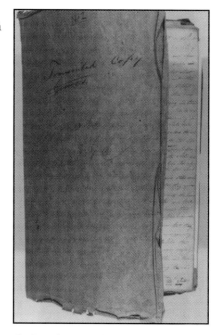

Joseph Smith Translation Manuscripts. Although Joseph Smith made notations in his Bible, the changes were actually recorded in manuscript form.

Eventually, Joseph completed the translation of the New Testament on 2 February 1833. The Lord informed the Prophet on 9 March 1833, "And when you have finished the translation of the prophets, you shall from thenceforth preside over the affairs of the church and the school [of the prophets]" (D&C 90:13). Shortly thereafter, Joseph came to the material known as the Apocrypha and received a revelation (D&C 91) that told him not to translate it.

Within a short time, the Lord asked Joseph to "hasten to translate" the scriptures (D&C 93:53). The next revelation stated that a lot near the Kirtland Temple lot should be reserved for another sacred building, "for the work of the printing of the translation of my scriptures" (D&C 94:10). By 2 July 1833, the manuscript of the Joseph Smith Translation (JST) concluded with the last chapter of the last book of the Old Testament, the book of Malachi.

The effort to publish the JST continued, and on 23 April 1834 Joseph received another revelation from the Lord indicating the Lord's desire that the translation be printed. "And for this purpose I have commanded you to organize yourselves, even to print my words, the fulness of my scriptures, the revelations which I have given unto you" (D&C 104:58). Following the difficult period of apostasy in Kirtland and the persecution in Missouri, the Saints gathered to Nauvoo, Illinois. The first canonized revelation recorded in Nauvoo picked up again on the theme of publishing the JST. Speaking of William Law, the Lord counseled, "If he will do my will let him from henceforth hearken to the counsel of my servant Joseph, and with his interest support the cause of the poor, and publish the new translation of my holy word unto the inhabitants of the earth" (D&C 124:89).

The JST was not published in the Prophet's lifetime, but Joseph's efforts in this "branch of his calling" had immense influence upon the revelations contained in the Doctrine and Covenants. Many sections were revealed as a direct result of the Prophet's work in translating the Bible.

THE NATURE OF REVELATION IN THE DOCTRINE AND COVENANTS

A CAREFUL EXAMINATION OF the Doctrine and Covenants demonstrates that Joseph Smith received revelations in diverse ways (for a fuller treatment of this subject, see Richard Neitzel Holzapfel, "Salvation Cannot Come without Revelation," in *Doctrines for Exaltation: The 1989 Sperry Symposium on the Doctrine and Covenants* [Salt Lake City: Deseret Book Co., 1989], pp. 87–96). During the Church's organizational meeting of 6 April 1830, Joseph Smith said that the "revelations of God . . . shall come hereafter by the gift and power of the Holy Ghost, the voice of God, or the ministering of angels" (D&C 20:35). While recording a revelation, the Prophet noted, "Thus saith the still small voice, which whispereth through and pierceth all things, and often times it maketh my bones to quake while it maketh manifest" (D&C 85:6). Apparently the physical impact of revelations varied also, for not always did Joseph's bones quake.

A few examples are found in the Doctrine and Covenants of revelations coming to Joseph Smith through a heavenly messenger. These instances include sections 2, 13, 27, and 110. Section 128, originally a letter, mentions the appearance of several other angelic ministers who came to Joseph.

Doctrine and Covenants revelations also came by vision. Only two examples of revelations received by Joseph Smith in this way are found in the Doctrine and Covenants. They are sections 76 and 137.

Several revelations were received through the use of divine instruments. Usually, the instrument was the seer stone or the Urim and Thummim. This method applies to sections 3, 6–7, 10–11, and 14–17. Doctrine and Covenants 130:14–15 records that Joseph heard a voice speak to him. This seems to be the only revelation in the Doctrine and Covenants given in this manner.

Of the 135 sections of the Doctrine and Covenants recorded during Joseph's lifetime, only 16 were received in these special ways. They were truly unusual events in Joseph's revelatory experience. An examination of revelation in ancient scripture seems to support this pattern. Modern and ancient scriptures testify that most often "the holy prophets . . . spake as they were inspired by the gift of the Holy Ghost" (D&C 20:26).

Most of the Doctrine and Covenants consists of revelations that God gave to Joseph Smith through the Holy Ghost. The Lord announced who he was and how he usually spoke to his servants when he said, "Behold, I, Jesus Christ, your Lord and your God, and your Redeemer, by the power of my Spirit have spoken it" (D&C 18:47). The Lord said that the voice Joseph Smith heard was "as the voice of one crying in the wilderness—in the wilderness, because you cannot see him—my voice, because my voice is Spirit; my Spirit is truth; truth abideth and hath no end; and if it be in you it shall abound" (D&C 88:66). Revelations given by the voice of the Spirit may include Doctrine and Covenants 1, 4–5, 8–9, 12, 18–26, 28–64, 66–73, 75, 78–101, 103–8, 111–12, 114–20, 122, 124–26, 129, and 132–33.

Doctrine and Covenants 65, 109, and 121 are revealed prayers (see *Times and Seasons* 5 [1 April 1844]: 482; see also *History of the Church* 2:420). Several other sections are Spirit-inspired letters (D&C 123; 127–28), minutes of a Church meeting (D&C 102), instructions (D&C 130–31), and questions and answers (D&C 77; 113). Initially, some of these were not considered revelations, but they became scripture as the Church came to value their contribution to Church members' understanding of important gospel principles. Nearly 88 percent of the Doctrine and Covenants consists of scripture given by the quiet inspiration of the Spirit of the Lord. A total of 124 of the 135 sections recorded during Joseph Smith's lifetime were received in this manner.

In May 1831, Joseph received a revelation in Thompson, Ohio (see D&C 51). Orson Pratt, who was present, later recalled, "No great noise or physical manifestation was made; Joseph was as calm as the morning sun" (quoted in Millennial Star 32 [11 August 1874]: 498).

Though the revelations were revealed by the Spirit, Joseph put the impressions in words. Orson Pratt said, "Joseph the Prophet, in writing the Doctrine and Covenants, received the ideas from God, but clothed those ideas with such words as came to his mind." Elder Pratt continued, "Had [modern scripture] been through Orson Pratt or John Taylor, probably different words would have been used by each one to convey the same meaning." (Minutes of the School of the Prophets, Salt Lake Stake, 9 December 1872, Archives Division, Church Historical Department, The Church of Jesus Christ of Latter-day Saints, Salt Lake City, Utah.)

Brigham Young made the following observation concerning language and revelation: "When God speaks to the people, he does it in a manner to suit their circumstances and capacities. He spoke to the children of Jacob through Moses, as a blind, stiff-necked people, and when Jesus and his Apostles came they talked with the Jews as a benighted, wicked, selfish people. They would not receive the Gospel, though presented to them by the Son of God in all its righteousness, beauty and glory. Should the Lord Almighty send an angel to re-write the Bible, it would in many places be very different from what it now is. And I will even venture to say that if the Book of Mormon were now to be re-written, in many instances it would materially differ from the present translation." (In *Journal of Discourses* 9:311.)

The Lord uses the language of the individual to reveal his mind and will (see D&C 1:24). In early Church history, some of the men around Joseph had more formal education than he. Some of them were concerned with the language Joseph used in the revelations. The Lord said, "Your eyes have been upon my servant Joseph Smith, Jun., and his language you have known, and his imperfections you have known; and you have sought in your hearts knowledge that you might express beyond his language" (D&C 67:5). These men were more concerned with the Church leader's language and grammar than with gospel messages revealed. The Lord's Spirit gave knowledge to Joseph, and Joseph put that knowledge into his own language so others could read it.

The canonized revelations of Brigham Young, Wilford Woodruff, Joseph F. Smith, and Spencer W. Kimball follow a similar pattern. Evidence suggests that "The Word and Will of the Lord" revealed to Brigham Young at Winter Quarters was a revelation of the Spirit, put into words by Brigham. Wilford Woodruff's Manifesto was a written document based on a visionary experience. Joseph F. Smith's "Vision of the Redemption of the Dead" was an open vision. The First Presidency's Official Declaration—2 is another written document in which the Spirit directed communication on 28 June 1978 to the question regarding priesthood ordination and temple worship.

Geographic Locations of the Revelations

For the vast majority of the Doctrine and Covenants revelations, a geographic location is known with certainty. In a few cases, however, the location is less certain, but we assume the revelation was given at or near the site specified in the "Chronological Order of Contents" section of the 1981 edition (see, for example, D&C 20, 32, 87, 104, and 113). In many cases, we know not only the town but also the home or building in which the revelation was recorded or received. (For overviews of Church historical sites in New York, Ohio, Missouri, Illinois, and southeastern Iowa, see the following books by Richard Neitzel Holzapfel and T. Jeffery Cottle— *Old Mormon Palmyra and New England: Historic Photographs and Guide* [Santa Ana, Calif.: Fieldbrook Productions, 1991]; *Old Mormon Kirtland and Missouri: Historic Photographs and Guide* [Santa Ana, Calif.: Fieldbrook Productions, 1991]; *Old Mormon Nauvoo and Southeastern Iowa: Historic Photographs and Guide* [Santa Ana, Calif.: Fieldbrook Productions, 1991].)

New York

Sometime in 1816, Joseph Smith, Sr., like many other New Englanders of the period, traveled west in search of a new beginning. He arrived in Palmyra Village, New York, a few weeks after his departure from Vermont. He left his family in Vermont to settle accounts and to prepare for their journey west to a new home. By 1818, he had accumulated enough money for the down payment on a hundred-acre woodland area in the Farmington township. During the first year, he and his sons cleared thirty acres of heavy timber, prepared the ground for cultivation, and planted wheat. By 1821, Joseph, Sr., had eleven children. He worked hard for his living. In 1822, Farmington township was divided, and the Smith farm became part of the newly created township of Manchester.

The family log cabin and nearby woods were the sites of Joseph Smith, Jr.'s, first revelations. The First Vision occurred in 1820 southwest from the family's first home. The angel Moroni appeared

Smith Home in Manchester, New York. This is where Doctrine and Covenants sections 2, 19, 22, and 23 were received.

to young Joseph in the upper floor or attic of the log cabin in 1823. The remaining revelations given in Manchester were received in the extant white frame home built across the road and just south of the original log cabin.

While living in Manchester, Ontario County, New York, Joseph received several revelations (see sections 2, 19, 22, and 23).

Section	Content
2	Moroni's teachings to Joseph
19	For Martin Harris: relationship of the Atonement and punishment
22	Old covenants done away; a new baptism is necessary
23	Duties of Oliver Cowdery, Joseph Knight, Sr., Hyrum, Samuel, and Joseph Smith, Sr.

The Church was founded in Fayette, Seneca County, New York, in 1830. Several revelations were received there before and after 6 April 1830 (see sections 14–18, 20–21, and 28–40). Most of the Book of Mormon was translated between April and June 1829 in Harmony, Pennsylvania. Struggling to complete the work in poor living conditions and in the face of local animosity, Joseph left Harmony around 1 June to live in the Whitmer home in Fayette.

Section	Content
14	For David Whitmer, who is to serve
15	For John Whitmer, who is to serve
16	For Peter Whitmer, Jr., who is to serve
17	For Oliver Cowdery; Three Witnesses designated
18	For Joseph Smith, Oliver Cowdery, and David Whitmer; the worth of souls is great
20	"Articles and Covenants of the Church"; beliefs and organization outlined
21	Joseph Smith is called to serve as seer, translator, prophet, Apostle, and elder
28	Hiram Page deceived; Oliver to go on a mission to the Lamanites
29	Information on the Second Coming
30	For David, Peter, Jr., and John Whitmer; Peter to go with Oliver on mission
31	For Thomas B. Marsh, who is to serve and follow counsel
32	For Parley P. Pratt and Ziba Peterson, who are to go on a Lamanite mission
33	For Ezra Thayer and Northrop Sweet, who are to serve in the eleventh hour
34	For Orson Pratt, who is to serve and prophesy
35	For Sidney Rigdon, who is to serve and act as scribe

Section	Content
36	For Edward Partridge, who is to serve with singleness of heart
37	The Bible translation to stop and the Saints to gather at "the Ohio"
38	Blessings await the Saints in Ohio
39	For James Covill to be baptized and to serve
40	The cares of the world allow persons (James Covill) to reject the message

After the Church headquarters were moved from New York to Kirtland, Ohio, Joseph Smith and other Church leaders and missionaries continued to travel throughout New York on Church business. In 1833, Joseph left his home on a "preaching journey." While his party visited at the home of "Father Nickerson" in Perrysburg, Cattaraugus County, New York, Joseph received one revelation (see section 100).

Section	Content
100	Sidney Rigdon to be an official spokesman

Pennsylvania

Joseph Smith, Jr., arrived in Harmony for the first time in November 1825. He and his father boarded at the Isaac Hale home during their brief employment with Josiah Stowell on a mining operation. Here he met his future wife, Emma Hale. Following their marriage, Joseph and Emma stayed briefly with the Smith family in Manchester, New York. Joseph and Emma went to Harmony to work on the translation of the Book of Mormon about December 1827. During their stay, Joseph accomplished most of the translation and received several important revelations and visitations (see sections 3–13 and 24–27).

Section	Content
3	Regarding the lost 116 translated pages from the book of Lehi
4	For Joseph Smith, Sr., to serve, as the "field is white"
5	For Martin Harris
6	For Oliver Cowdery, to serve as scribe
7	A part of a lost parchment of John the Apostle
8	For Oliver Cowdery, regarding the "gift of translation"
9	For Oliver Cowdery, to continue as scribe; reason for loss of gifts
10	For Joseph Smith, who is not to retranslate the book of Lehi

Section	Content
11	For Hyrum Smith, who is to serve and prepare to preach
12	For Joseph Knight, Sr., who is to serve and help establish Zion
13	Joseph and Oliver receive the Aaronic Priesthood from John the Baptist
24	For Joseph Smith, Oliver Cowdery, and elders who should magnify offices
25	For Emma Smith, who is to serve and to compile a Church hymnal
26	For Joseph and Oliver, the law of common consent is affirmed
27	For Joseph and the Church; other foods and drinks, besides bread and wine, are suitable for the sacrament—what counts is righteous motives

Massachusetts

In 1836, Joseph Smith, Oliver Cowdery, and Sidney Rigdon arrived in Salem. While attending to Church business, the Prophet Joseph received one revelation (see section 111).

Section	Content
111	For Joseph, more treasure than one in Salem

Ohio

Following his departure from New York to "the Ohio," Joseph began to receive a number of revelations now found in the Doctrine and Covenants. Some of the most important revelations of the period were received in the homes and in the public and Church buildings of Kirtland, Hiram, Amherst, and Orange, Ohio.

Kirtland, Ohio, was the Church headquarters and site of the first completed temple. While living and working in the area, Joseph received several significant revelations (see sections 41–50, 52–56, 63–64, 70, 72, 84–98, 101–4, 106–10, 112, 134, and 137).

Section	Content
41	For the Church, Edward Partridge is called as the first bishop
42	The law of the Church, consecration, discipline, and the Ten Commandments reviewed
43	For the Church, Joseph is the only one ordained to receive revelations for the Church

Section	Content
44	For the elders of the Church, who are called to Kirtland for a conference
45	Signs of the Second Coming reviewed
46	The gifts of the Spirit outlined
47	For John Whitmer, who is to serve as the first Church historian
48	Ohio Saints to help New York Saints purchase land in Kirtland region
49	For Sidney Rigdon, Parley P. Pratt, and Leman Copley, who are to preach to the Shakers
50	For the Church, many false spirits
52	Elders called to travel to Missouri for next Church conference
53	For A. Sidney Gilbert, who is called to forsake the world
54	For Colesville Saints, who are to relocate in Missouri
55	For William W. Phelps, who is to serve and help publish Church-related material
56	For Thomas B. Marsh, the law of revocation explained
63	The Saints to gather in western Missouri; using the Lord's name in vain explained
64	Joseph Smith has "keys of the mysteries"; the law of forgiveness explained
70	For members of the Literary Firm; scriptures to be published
72	Newel K. Whitney called as bishop; his duties revealed
84	"The Revelation on Priesthood," including the oath and covenant of the priesthood
85	Extracts from a letter, including instructions given by the Spirit
86	Parable of the wheat and tares interpreted and information on lineal rights reviewed
87	"The Prophecy on War" regarding the Northern and Southern states
88	"The Olive Leaf" regarding the building of the temple and attendant meetings and ordinances
89	"The Word of Wisdom"
90	Sidney Rigdon and Frederick G. Williams called to the Presidency along with Joseph

Section	Content
91	Joseph Smith is not to translate the Apocrypha
92	For Frederick G. Williams, who is to become a member of the united order
93	Faithful Saints shall see God; the glory of God is intelligence
94	Church administration offices to be built under direction of Hyrum Smith and others
95	Church members reproved for lack of progress on the Kirtland Temple
96	Newel K. Whitney to take charge of the Peter French farm in Kirtland
97	For the Lord's friends; Kirtland is to become strong
98	Constitutional law of the land to be observed; law of forgiveness and retribution reviewed
101	Explanation of why the Jackson County Saints were driven out; United States Constitution inspired
102	Minutes of the organization of the high council; procedural items revealed
103	Revelation on the redemption of Zion; volunteers for Zion's Camp called
104	The united order reorganized in Missouri
106	For Warren Cowdery, who is to serve and preside over Freedom, New York, Branch
107	"The Revelation on Priesthood"; two priesthoods and five governing councils
108	For Lyman Sherman, who will be blessed if faithful; "strengthen your brethren"
109	Prayer of dedication for the Kirtland Temple
110	Joseph and Oliver's 1836 vision of Christ and other angelic ministers in the temple
112	For the Twelve Apostles
134	Statement regarding governments, probably written by Oliver Cowdery
137	Joseph Smith's 1836 "Vision of the Celestial Kingdom"

While visiting Thompson, Ohio, Joseph recorded one revelation (see section 51).

Section	Content
51	For Edward Partridge, who is to regulate

Section	Content
	stewardship; instructions on consecration revealed

John Johnson Home, Hiram, Ohio. A significant number of revelations were received here.

Hiram, Ohio, was the home of Joseph and Emma during a very critical time in Church history. Some of the most significant revelations recorded during the Ohio period were received at the John Johnson farmhouse (see sections, 1, 65, 67–69, 71, 73–74, 76–81, 99, and 133).

Section	Content
1	The "Preface" to the Book of Commandments, introducing the revelations
65	Keys of the kingdom are upon the earth
67	The Lord's challenge to duplicate the least of Joseph's revelations
68	Revelation regarding the Holy Spirit and scripture
69	John Whitmer and Oliver Cowdery to take the revelations to Missouri to be printed
71	Joseph and Sidney to meet their enemies, who will be confounded
73	Joseph and Sidney to continue the translation of the Bible
74	Explanation of Paul's instruction to the Corinthian Saints (1 Corinthians 7:14)
76	"The Vision," identifying the three degrees of glory
77	Explanation of certain passages in the book of Revelation
78	A storehouse to be established among the Saints
79	For Jared Carter, who is to serve
80	For Stephen Burnett and Eden Smith, who are to serve
81	For Jesse Gause, who is to serve in the Presidency

Section	Content
99	For John Murdock, who is to serve; "those that receive you, receive me"
133	"The Appendix"; the Saints should prepare for the Second Coming

Joseph Smith received a revelation in Orange, Ohio, while attending to matters of Church business during a conference (see section 66). This meeting was held in the home of Sirenus Burnett.

Section	Content
66	For William E. McLellin, who is to serve and preach

While visiting members of the Church in Amherst, Ohio, Joseph received a revelation (see section 75).

Section	Content
75	Elders to serve as missionaries and families to receive help from Church

Missouri

The Saints built two Church centers during the 1830s, one in Ohio and another in Missouri. Joseph Smith viewed Missouri as a new land of promise—the site of the gathering to build the New Jerusalem. The Saints were told in June 1831 that the land of their inheritance would be revealed to them as soon as their leader went to Missouri. The desire to build Zion—the ideal community mentioned in ancient biblical and modern scriptures—permeated the lives of the Saints during their early history. Within ten years, the Saints had sought to establish three major Church centers in Missouri—in Jackson County, 1831–33; in the adjoining counties, including Clay and Ray counties, 1833–36; and in the northern counties of Caldwell, Carroll, and Daviess, 1836–39.

The Prophet Joseph never lived in Jackson County, Missouri, identified as the center place by revelation, but during his visits there, he received several significant revelations (see sections 57–60 and 82–83).

Section	Content
57	The Saints are to gather to Zion (Missouri); Independence is the "center place"
58	Laws of the land are to be obeyed; Saints should be "anxiously engaged"
59	Blessings of faithfully observing the Sabbath
60	Elders to return to Ohio and preach along the way

Section	Content
82	A united order to be established in Jackson County; where much is given, much is required
83	Rights of widows and children reviewed

Upon his return to Kirtland after a visit to Jackson County, Joseph received two revelations along the Missouri River, Missouri (see sections 61–62). The first was received at McLlwaine's Bend (near present Miami, Saline County, Missouri) and the second at Chariton, Chariton County, Missouri.

Section	Content
61	Dangers of traveling upon the waters; let the Spirit guide in travel
62	Elders to continue their mission; testimonies recorded in heaven

At the end of their long march from Ohio, Zion's Camp stopped at Fishing River, Missouri. Here Joseph Smith received a revelation (see section 105).

Section	Content
105	Why Zion could not be redeemed at that time

The Church headquarters were moved from Kirtland to Far West, Missouri. While living in Far West, Joseph received several revelations (see sections 113–15 and 117–20).

Section	Content
113	Answers to questions on certain Isaiah passages
114	For David Patten, who is to leave on a mission to the British Isles
115	The official name of the Church revealed; temple to be built at Far West, Missouri
117	Matters regarding Kirtland are to be resolved
118	Reorganization of the Quorum of the Twelve
119	Revelation on tithing and surplus
120	The Presidency, Bishopric, and High Council should work together on financial matters

Not far from the site of Far West, Joseph received a revelation at Spring Hill, Daviess County, Missouri (see section 116).

Section	Content
116	Spring Hill is identified as Adam-ondi-Ahman

While in jail in Liberty, Clay County, Missouri, Joseph wrote several letters of counsel to his family and to the Church. Among these letters are some of the Lord's most penetrating words (see sections 121–23).

Liberty Jail, Liberty, Missouri. This is where Joseph Smith wrote two letters that are now contained in Doctrine and Covenants 121–23.

Section	Content
121	Joseph pleads for deliverance and for the suffering Saints; revelation on righteousness
122	Joseph's persecution; suffering is "for thy good"
123	Saints are enjoined to collect information regarding their sufferings

Illinois

Following their expulsion from Missouri, the Saints began to gather in Illinois (and on the eastern shore of the Mississippi River in Iowa) to build another temple city—Nauvoo. During the Nauvoo period (1839–46), very few written revelations were recorded and published. Earlier, the written revelations had been a major vehicle to establish the Church's organization. However, as Joseph Smith and the Saints matured in spiritual matters, a letter or spoken communication often sufficed to reveal the mind of the Lord. The 1840s, as well as bringing increased interest among the Saints, brought a sense of urgency to Joseph for expounding the doctrinal implications of the Restoration. As a result, Joseph's written revelations largely gave way to public sermons, official newspaper editorials, and letters.

In Nauvoo, Hancock County, Illinois, several written revelations were recorded. A few were official letters that eventually took on the authority of scripture, much like the New Testament Epistles did for the early Christian church (see sections 124–29, 132, and 135).

Edward Hunter Home, Nauvoo, Illinois. Because of threats of unlawful arrest, Joseph Smith was in hiding in the Hunter home. While there, he wrote a letter regarding baptism for the dead. This letter was incorporated into Doctrine and Covenants 128.

Section	Content
124	Major organizational revelation and official call to build the Nauvoo Temple
125	Saints to build up the Iowa settlements of Zarahemla and Nashville
126	For Brigham Young, who is commended for his labors and is called to remain at home
127	Letter from Joseph Smith regarding work for the dead
128	Letter from Joseph Smith regarding work for the dead
129	Three grand keys given to detect false spirits
132	Revelation on eternal sealings, including laws governing plural marriage
135	John Taylor's account of the murders of Joseph and Hyrum Smith

An important Church branch was located at Ramus, Hancock County, Illinois. Here Joseph stopped on several occasions to visit family members, friends, and Church leaders. Some of Joseph's inspired instructions were canonized (see sections 130–31).

Section	Content
130	Instructions given by Joseph Smith on

Section	Content
	various subjects: Godhead, knowledge, and obedience
131	Instructions given by Joseph Smith on eternal marriage and more sure word of prophecy

Winter Quarters, Nebraska

The Saints began to gather at the Missouri River in 1846–47 in preparation for the long trek to the Rocky Mountains. While in Winter Quarters, Nebraska, Brigham Young received several revelations, dreams, and visions. One revelation given to Brigham Young during this period was published and included in the Doctrine and Covenants as section 136. (A comprehensive treatment of the Winter Quarters period is found in Richard E. Bennett, *Mormons at the Missouri, 1846–1852: "And Should We Die . . ."* [Norman: University of Oklahoma Press, 1987].)

Section	Content
136	Revelation through Brigham Young regarding the Saints' emigration west

Salt Lake City, Utah

The Saints eventually gathered in the Rocky Mountains. Under the direction of Brigham Young, they expanded their geographical kingdom. During the remainder of the nineteenth century and in the twentieth century, many of the succeeding prophets' revelations and visions concerning the Church were recorded and published. A few were included as part of the Doctrine and Covenants, though some only temporarily.

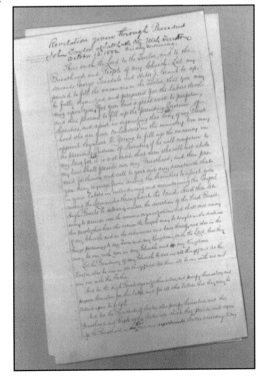

Manuscript of John Taylor's 1882 Revelation. L. John Nuttall, a secretary to President John Taylor, recorded an important administrative revelation given to President Taylor on 13 October 1882. The revelation called George Teasdale and Heber J. Grant to fill vacancies in the Quorum of the Twelve. This revelation, along with a second revelation recorded the following year, were first published in several foreign-language editions of the Doctrine and Covenants.

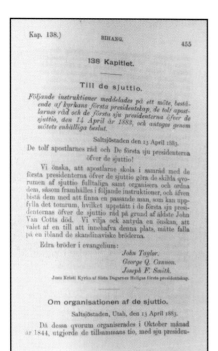

1888 Swedish Doctrine and Covenants with John Taylor's Revelation. Several foreign-language editions of the Doctrine and Covenants included two of President John Taylor's revelations (received in 1882 and 1883). These revelations were never officially canonized or published in an English-language edition of the Doctrine and Covenants.

In Salt Lake City, Salt Lake County, Utah, three important items were received as revelations from the Lord (see section 138 and Official Declarations—1–2).

Section	Content
138	Joseph F. Smith's 1918 "Vision of the Redemption of the Dead"
Official Declaration—1	Wilford Woodruff's 1890 Manifesto on plural marriage
Official Declaration—2	The First Presidency's 1978 public announcement regarding priesthood

1890 Manifesto Pamphlet. On 24 September 1890, President Wilford Woodruff showed fellow Church leaders a document regarding the ending of plural marriage. The document was approved and prepared for publication, and the Manifesto was released to the nation's newspapers on the following day. Eventually, this notice was published in the 1908 Doctrine and Covenants, and in 1981, historical background material was added.

James E. Talmage's Diary Entry for 31 October 1918. Following the Church's semiannual general conference, Joseph F. Smith submitted to the members of the First Presidency and Council of the Twelve a vision he received on 3 October 1918. They unanimously accepted it as revelation. In 1976, this vision was officially added to the standard works of the Church and soon afterward was designated as section 138 in the Doctrine and Covenants.

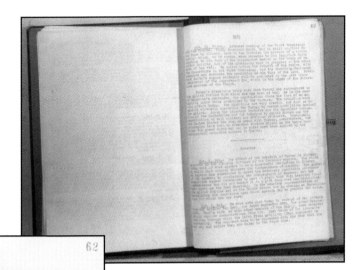

The Book of Covenants, as the Doctrine and Covenants was called by the early Saints, stands as a witness that God and Jesus Christ live.

Brigham Young noted, "Most of the revelations he [Joseph] received in the early part of his ministry pertained to what the few around him should do in this or in that case—when and how they should perform their duties" (in *Journal of Discourses* 6:171). Though given to individuals and in most cases in settings very different from the ones we live in today, the revelations are still relevant. In section 25, the Lord speaks specifically to Emma Smith but ends the revelation with the words, "And verily, verily, I say unto you, that this is my voice unto all. Amen." (D&C 25:16.) On another occasion, when calling Edward Partridge to serve, the Lord said, "And now this calling and commandment give I unto you concerning all men" (D&C 36:4). What makes scripture so enduring is the fact that applications are innumerable and span all distances of time and space. The Lord counsels his children to benefit from revelations and commandments (see D&C 70:3, 8).

> ***First Presidency Letter (8 June 1978).*** As a result of a revelation received in the Salt Lake Temple, Spencer W. Kimball and his counselors in the First Presidency issued a letter informing the Church and the world of a momentous change in Church policy. The letter was included in the 1981 Doctrine and Covenants under the title, "Official Declaration—2."

Although a vast majority of the revelations contained in the Doctrine and Covenants deal with the administration and organization of the Church during the first decade of its existence, these revelations remain the "foundation of the Church" and the "salvation of the world." As the Prophet Joseph Smith testified, they contain the "keys of the mysteries of the Kingdom" and the "riches of eternity." (Far West Record, 12–13 November 1831, Archives Division, Church Historical Department, The Church of Jesus Christ of Latter-day Saints, Salt Lake City, Utah; see Donald Q. Cannon and Lyndon W. Cook, eds., *Far West Record* [Salt Lake City: Deseret Book Co., 1983], p. 32.)

SELECT BIBLIOGRAPHY

Anderson, Carma de Jong. "A Historical Overview of the Mormons and Their Clothing, 1840–1850." Ph.D. diss., Brigham Young University, 1992.

Anderson, Karl Ricks. *Joseph Smith's Kirtland: Eyewitness Accounts*. Salt Lake City: Deseret Book Co., 1989.

Backman, Milton V., Jr. *The Heavens Resound: A History of the Latter-day Saints in Ohio, 1830–1838*. Salt Lake City: Deseret Book Co., 1983.

Barry, James P. *Ships of the Great Lakes: 300 Years of Navigation*. Berkeley: Howell-North Books, 1973.

Bennett, Richard E. *Mormons at the Missouri, 1846–1852: "And Should We Die . . ."* Norman: University of Oklahoma Press, 1987.

Bitton, Davis. "The Waning of Mormon Kirtland." *BYU Studies* 12 (Summer 1972): 455–64.

Bray, Robert T. *The Turley Site: An Account of the 1973 Archaeological Work, Nauvoo, Illinois*. Columbia: University of Missouri Press, 1980.

Bushman, Richard L. *Joseph Smith and the Beginnings of Mormonism*. Urbana: University of Illinois Press, 1984.

Cannon, Donald Q. "Licensing in the Early Church." *BYU Studies* 22 (Winter 1982): 96–105.

Cannon, Donald Q., and Lyndon W. Cook, eds. *Far West Record*. Salt Lake City: Deseret Book Co., 1983.

Cook, Lyndon W. *The Revelations of the Prophet Joseph Smith: A Historical and Biographical Commentary of the Doctrine and Covenants*. Salt Lake City: Deseret Book Co., 1985.

Crawley, Peter. "Joseph Smith and a *Book of Commandments*." *Princeton University Library Chronicle* 42 (Autumn 1980): 18–32.

Demos, John. *A Little Commonwealth: Family Life in Plymouth Colony*. New York: Oxford University Press, 1970.

Flake, Chad J. "The Newell K. Whitney Collection." *BYU Studies* 11 (Summer 1971): 322–28.

———, ed. *A Mormon Bibliography, 1830–1930*. Salt Lake City: University of Utah Press, 1978.

Flake, Chad J., and Larry W. Draper, comps. *A Mormon Bibliography, 1830–1930, Ten-Year Supplement*. Salt Lake City: University of Utah Press, 1989.

Givens, George W. *In Old Nauvoo*. Salt Lake City: Deseret Book Co., 1990.

Harrington, Virginia S., and J. C. Harrington. *Rediscovery of the Nauvoo Temple: Report on Archaeological Excavations*. Salt Lake City: Nauvoo Restoration, Inc., 1971.

Hayden, Dolores. *Seven American Utopias: The Architecture of Communitarian Socialism, 1790–1975*. Cambridge: MIT Press, 1976.

Holzapfel, Richard Neitzel. "Salvation Cannot Come without Revelation." In *Doctrines for Exaltation: The 1989 Sperry Symposium on the Doctrine and Covenants*, pp. 87–96. Salt Lake City: Deseret Book Co., 1989.

Holzapfel, Richard Neitzel, and T. Jeffery Cottle. *Old Mormon Kirtland and Missouri: Historic Photographs and Guide*. Santa Ana, Calif.: Fieldbrook Productions, 1991.

———. *Old Mormon Nauvoo and Southeastern Iowa: Historic Photographs and Guide*. Santa Ana, Calif.: Fieldbrook Productions, 1991.

———. *Old Mormon Palmyra and New England: Historic Photographs and Guide*. Santa Ana, Calif.: Fieldbrook Productions, 1991.

Kalman, Bobbie. *Early Settler Life Series*. New York: Crabtree Publishing Co., 1983–91.

Kimball, Stanley B. "Missouri Mormon Manuscripts: Sources in Selected Societies." *BYU Studies* 14 (Summer 1974): 458–87.

Mackay, Charles. *The Mormons, or Latter-day Saints*. London: Office of National Illustrated Library, 1852.

Madden, Betty I. *Arts, Crafts and Architecture in Early Illinois*. Urbana: University of Illinois Press, 1974.

Olsen, Steven L., and Dale F. Beecher. *Presidents of the Church*. Salt Lake City: Museum of Church History and Art, The Church of Jesus Christ of Latter-day Saints, 1985.

Olson, Earl E. "The Chronology of the Ohio Revelations." *BYU Studies* 11 (Summer 1971): 329–49.

Partridge, Scott H. "The Failure of the Kirtland Safety Society." *BYU Studies* 12 (Summer 1972): 437–54.

Penney, David W. *Art of the American Indian Frontier*. Seattle: University of Washington Press, 1992.

Petersen, Melvin J. "Preparing Early Revelations for Publication." *Ensign* 15 (February 1985): 14–20.

Rust, Alvin E. *Mormon and Utah Coin and Currency*. Salt Lake City: Rust Rare Coins, Inc., 1984.

Schlereth, Thomas J., ed. *Material Culture: A Research Guide*. Lawrence: University Press of Kansas, 1985.

Smith, Joseph. *History of The Church of Jesus Christ of Latter-day Saints*. Edited by B. H. Roberts. 7 vols. Salt Lake City: The Church of Jesus Christ of Latter-day Saints, 1932–51.

———. *Teachings of the Prophet Joseph Smith*. Selected by Joseph Fielding Smith. Salt Lake City: Deseret Book Co., 1938.

White, John H., Jr. *American Locomotives: An Engineering History, 1830–1880*. Baltimore: John Hopkins Press, 1968.

Woodford, Robert J. "The Historical Development of the Doctrine and Covenants." Ph.D. diss., Brigham Young University, 1974.

———. "How the Revelations in the Doctrine and Covenants Were Received and Compiled." *Ensign* 15 (January 1985): 27–33.

———. "The Story of the Doctrine and Covenants." *Ensign* 14 (December 1984): 32–39.

Woodward, Charles L. *Bibliothica-scallawagiana*. New York, 1880.

SOURCES OF PHOTOGRAPHS/ARTIFACTS

The abbreviations listed below have been used to simplify references in the sources that follow:

DIA — Detroit Institute of Arts, Detroit, Michigan

DUP — The National Society Daughters of Utah Pioneers Memorial Museum, Salt Lake City, Utah

HBLLBYU — Manuscript Department, Special Collections, and Photoarchives, Harold B. Lee Library, Brigham Young University, Provo, Utah

LDS Church Archives — Archives Division, Church Historical Department, The Church of Jesus Christ of Latter-day Saints, Salt Lake City, Utah

MCHA — Museum of Church History and Art, The Church of Jesus Christ of Latter-day Saints, Salt Lake City, Utah

NRI — Nauvoo Restoration, Inc., Nauvoo, Illinois

RLDSLA — Library-Archives and Museum, Reorganized Church of Jesus Christ of Latter Day Saints, World Headquarters, Independence, Missouri

RTF — Restoration Trails Foundation, Independence, Missouri

VRL — Visual Resources Library, The Church of Jesus Christ of Latter-day Saints, Salt Lake City, Utah

---

FRONT COVER

Joseph Smith Portrait, ca. 1842. (Oil portrait.) Courtesy of First Presidency, Reorganized Church of Jesus Christ of Latter Day Saints, World Headquarters, Independence, Missouri.

Josiah Butterfield's Seventies Quorum Belt Buckle. (Such belt buckles were made for use by Presidents of the First Quorum of Seventies.) RTF.

Delaware or Shawnee Indian Coat. DIA.

Hyrum Smith's Sunglasses and Case. (Glasses used to correct farsightedness.) Eldred G. Smith Family Collection.

Phoebe Carter Woodruff's Ring. (Given to her by Wilford Woodruff early in their marriage.) MCHA.

Emma Smith's Side Table. (Made from birch and mahogany.) MCHA.

Joseph Smith's Nauvoo Legion Pistol. MCHA.

BACK COVER

       Hyrum Smith's Nauvoo Legion Sword. Eldred G. Smith Family Collection.
       Mary Fielding Smith's Shawl. MCHA.
       Key for the Carthage Jail. RLDSLA.
       First Edition (1830) of the Book of Mormon. MCHA.
       Hand-forged Fireplace Shovel Made by Brigham Young. MCHA.
       Julia Smith Middleton's Purse. RLDSLA.
       1843 Five-dollar Gold Piece Used in Nauvoo. RLDSLA.
       Lap Desk Toolbox in Which Joseph Smith Hid the Gold Plates. Eldred G.
          Smith Family Collection.

SECTION ONE
EARLY LATTER-DAY SAINT TEMPLES

Page 3   *Nauvoo Temple Donation Box.* NRI.

INDEPENDENCE TEMPLE

   Page 4   *Independence (Zion) Plat Map.* LDS Church Archives.
              Temple Site Marker. LDS Church Archives.

   Page 5   *Newel K. Whitney's Map Containers.* MCHA.
              Independence Temple Drawing. LDS Church Archives.

FAR WEST TEMPLE

   Page 6   *1838 Far West Plat Map.* MCHA.

   Page 7   *Far West Temple Cornerstone.* RLDSLA.
              Wilford Woodruff's Journal, 26 April 1839. LDS Church Archives.

KIRTLAND TEMPLE

   Page 8   *Kirtland Temple.* RLDSLA.
              Emer Harris's Square. MCHA.

   Page 9   *Kirtland Temple Window.* VRL.
              Temple Curtain Pulleys. RLDSLA.
              West Pulpit of the Lower Assembly Room. Library of Congress, Washington,
                 D.C.
              Kirtland Temple Step Stone. Private possession.

NAUVOO TEMPLE

   Page 10   *Nauvoo Temple Architect's Drawing.* MCHA.

Page 11   *Alpheus Cutler's Building Tools.* RTF.
           Nauvoo Temple Limestone. Private collection.
           Francis Clark's Spiral Template and Drafting Tools. MCHA.

Page 12   *Star Stone from the Nauvoo Temple.* Harold Allen, Chicago, Illinois.
           Part of Stone Oxen from Baptismal Font. MCHA.
           Nauvoo Temple Sacrament Cup. MCHA.
           Thomas Easterly's Daguerreotype of the Temple. Archives-Library, Missouri
              Historical Society, St. Louis, Missouri.
           Nauvoo Temple Key. RLDSLA.

SECTION TWO
SOCIAL SETTINGS IN EARLY CHURCH HISTORY

Page 13   *Windsor-Style Chair Used in Newel K. Whitney's Store in Kirtland, Ohio.*
              MCHA.
           Mangle Board (Used for Smoothing Out Damp Linen or Cloth). MCHA.
           Early Trunk. MCHA.
           *School Bell Used by Joseph Smith, Sr. (Also Used as a Family Dinner Bell by
              Lucy Mack Smith.)* Eldred G. Smith Family Collection.
           Candle Snuffer. MCHA.

ESTABLISHING A HOME

Page 14   *Joseph Smith's Axe Head.* RLDSLA.
           Howard and Martha Knowlton Coray's Log Cabin. Nauvoo Historical Society,
              Nauvoo, Illinois.

Page 15   *Fireplace Swing Crane.* RTF.
           Water-Bucket Carrier. RTF.
           The Noble–Lucy Mack Smith Home Latrine. LDS Church Archives.
           Nauvoo Pitcher. RTF.

Page 16   *A Stool Used in the Smith Family Cabin.* Eldred G. Smith Family Collection.
           Wood and Rope Bed. NRI.

PRINTING AND PUBLISHING

Page 17   *Martin Harris's 1830 Copy of the Book of Mormon.* MCHA.
           Inkwell. RTF.
           The Grandin Print Shop. LDS Church Archives.

Page 18   *Grandin's "Smith Patented Improved Press."* VRL.
           Original Manuscript of the Book of Mormon. VRL.
           Printer's Copy of the Manuscript of the Book of Mormon. RLDSLA.

Page 19   *Type from the Grandin Printing Shop.* VRL.
          Printer Page Proof Sheet. MCHA.
          Signature of the Book of Mormon. MCHA.
          Reflector, 2 January 1830. HBLLBYU.

WOMEN AND CHILDREN

Page 20   *Baby Clothes, Socks, Cap, and Cradle.* RTF.

Page 21   *Marbles and Doll Used in Nauvoo,* DUP.
          Rocking Horse Used by the Saints' Children in Nauvoo. NRI.
          Slate Tablet and Slate Pencil. RTF.

Page 22   *Candle Maker Used in Nauvoo.* RTF.
          *Perfume Bottle from Nauvoo, Cosmetic Container, and Gold Bead from a
              Necklace.* RTF and RLDSLA.
          Relief Society Donation Box, Pennies, Nails, and Temple Glass. MCHA,
              private possession, and NRI.

MUSIC AND WORSHIP

Page 23   *Clarinet.* MCHA.
          Harmonica Plate from Nauvoo. RTF.
          Violin and Case. MCHA.

Page 24   *Bugle.* MCHA.
          The Evening and the Morning Star. HBLLBYU.
          Pewter Sacrament Cup Used in Nauvoo. DUP.
          1835 Church Hymnal. RLDSLA.
          Cello and Bow. MCHA.

VILLAGE AND FAMILY LIFE

Page 25   *1838 Plat Map of Adam-ondi-Ahman (Missouri).* LDS Church Archives.
          Brigham Young's Wood Plainer, Ruler, and Promissory Note. VRL.

Page 26   *Nauvoo Mansion House Rain Gutter.* MCHA.
          Top Quilt. RTF.
          Chair Made by Brigham Young. MCHA.
          Toothbrush Handle, Hair Curler, Combs, and Hair Grease Container. NRI; RTF.

BANKING AND ECONOMICS

Page 27   *Kirtland Safety Society Bank.* LDS Church Archives.

Page 28   *Kirtland Safety Society Bank Note.* Private collection, R. Q. Shupe, Capistrano,
          California.

Kirtland Safety Society Anti-Bank Note. Private collection, R. Q. Shupe, Capistrano, California.
Period United States Coinage. Private collection.
Kirtland Safety Society Bank Iron Safe. Western Reserve Historical Society Museum, Cleveland, Ohio.

Page 29   *Early 1830s Stewardship Agreement.* LDS Church Archives.
Nauvoo House Association Notes (First Issue). HBLLBYU.
Nauvoo City Scrip. HBLLBYU.

TRANSPORTATION

Page 30   *Ohio-Erie Canal.* Western Reserve Historical Society Museum, Cleveland, Ohio.
Horse Saddle. DUP.

Page 31   *Nineteenth-Century Sleigh.* DUP.
Nineteenth-Century Ship's Bell. British Museum, London, England.
List of Provisions Handbill. LDS Church Archives.
The Ship Britannia. Mariners Museum, Newport News, Virginia.
Hardtack (Sea Biscuit). National Maritime Museum, Greenwich, England.

Page 32   *Mississippi River Steamboat.* Cincinnati Public Library, Cincinnati, Ohio.
1838 Baltimore and Ohio's No. 16 Locomotive. Photo Archives, Smithsonian Institute, Washington, D.C.

FRONTIER LIFE AND AMUSEMENTS

Page 33   *Musket Bullet.* Private possession.
Joseph Smith's Top Hat and Case. RTF.
Emma Smith's Riding Crop. RTF.

Page 34   *Wilford Woodruff's Fishing Pole.* MCHA.
Children's Toy Bear from Nauvoo. NRI.
Playbill from Nauvoo. Archives-Library, Missouri Historical Society, St. Louis, Missouri.
Dominoes Used in Nauvoo. NRI.

CLOTHING AND TEXTILES

Page 35   *Scissors and Thimble from Nauvoo.* NRI.
Emma Smith's Spinning Wheel. VRL.

Page 36   *Lucy Mack Smith's Silk Bonnet.* RLDSLA.
Buttons Used in Nauvoo. VRL.
Hyrum Smith's Wool Pants. Eldred G. Smith Family Collection.
William Marks's Wool and Linen Vest. RLDSLA.

Emma Smith's Apron. RLDSLA.
Iron from Nauvoo. NRI.

COMMUNICATION AND NEWS

Page 37   **Times and Seasons *Newspaper.*** RLDSLA.
         Webb Post Office Box Drawer from Nauvoo. NRI.

Page 38   *Letter from Joseph Smith to Emma Smith (13 October 1832).* LDS Church
         Archives.
         Book of Mormon Broadside (Broadsheet). VRL.
         Candle Holders Used in Nauvoo. RTF.
         Far West Postmark. LDS Church Archives.
         The Newel K. Whitney Store. LDS Church Archives.

MISSIONARIES

Page 39   *Joseph Smith's Cloak.* VRL.
         Missionary Handbill. LDS Church Archives.

Page 40   **Missionary Certificate.** HBLLBYU.
         David Whitmer's Trunk. VRL.
         Manuscript Copy of Doctrine and Covenants, Section 5. HBLLBYU.
         W. W. Phelps's Missionary Journal. MCHA.

FOOD AND MEDICINE

Page 41   **Plow from Nauvoo.** DUP.
         Hoe Head Used in Nauvoo. NRI.
         Corn Husker. RLDSLA.

Page 42   **Times and Seasons *Advertisement.*** Private possession, R. Q. Shupe, Capistrano,
         California.
         *Earthenware, Including a Plate and Mug Belonging to Joseph and Emma
         Smith.* RTF.
         Stoneware Used in Nauvoo. RTF.

Page 43   *Utensils Used by the Saints.* VRL.
         Mortar and Pestle. RLDSLA.
         Pill Maker. NRI.
         Tooth Puller. NRI.

MILITARY AND WEAPONS

Page 44   *David W. Patten's Horn, Pouch, and Rifle.* MCHA.
         Nauvoo City Charter, Which Contained the Ordinances of the Nauvoo Legion.
         HBLLBYU.

Page 45   *Simple Shot Pistol, Box, Ball, Powder, and Pouch of Newel K. Whitney.* MCHA.
    Stiletto and Sheath. RLDSLA.
    Joseph Smith's Nauvoo Uniform Epaulet and Sash. RLDSLA.
    Sow Cannon Used by the Nauvoo Legion. MCHA.
    Nauvoo Legion Sword and Scabbard. RLDSLA.

LAMANITES

Page 46   *Lithograph by John McGahey of Joseph Smith Preaching to the Indians.* Illinois State Historical Library, Springfield, Illinois.
    Covenant of Lamanite Missionaries from the Ravenna, Ohio Star. HBLLBYU.

Page 47   *Iroquois Moccasins.* DIA.
    Potawatomi Headdress. DIA.
    Knife and Sheath. DIA.
    Ottawa Presentation Tomahawk. DIA.
    Potawatomi Garter. DIA.

COURTS AND JAILS

Page 48   *The Carthage Jail.* LDS Church Archives.
    Handcuffs from Nauvoo. NRI.
    Liberty Jail Window Bars. MCHA.
    Liberty Jail Door. RLDSLA.

Page 49   *Circuit Court Order.* Missouri State Historical Society, Columbia, Missouri.
    Joseph Smith's Letter from Liberty Jail. VRL.
    Liberty Jail Stone Floor. RLDSLA.
    The Liberty Jail. LDS Church Archives.

WRITINGS, RECORDS, AND BOOKS

Page 50   *Joseph Smith's Diary—1832–1834.* VRL.
    Quill and Ink. RTF.

Page 51   *Kirtland Revelation Book.* LDS Church Archives.
    Smith Family Bible. VRL.
    Nauvoo House Cornerstone. HBLLBYU.
    Relief Society Minute Book. LDS Church Archives.
    John Whitmer's History. RLDSLA.

MERCANTILE

Page 52   *Newel K. Whitney's Lap Desk.* MCHA.
    Newel K. Whitney's Store Ledger Book. MCHA.
    Joseph Smith's Office Sign from the Red Brick Store. MCHA.

Page 53   *Steelyard Weigh Scale.* NRI.
                           Nauvoo Blacksmith's Anvil. NRI.
                           Glass Pitcher. MCHA.
                           Soldering Iron from Nauvoo. NRI.
                           Willard Richards's Grooming Kit. MCHA.
                           Haun's Mill Face Wheel. MCHA.

ARCHITECTS, BUILDERS, AND CRAFTSMEN

Page 54   *Nauvoo Compass.* RTF.
                           Brick from a Nauvoo Home. Private possession.
                           Floor Plans for the Red Brick Store. HBLLBYU.

Page 55   *Plainers, Drill, Auger, and Trowel.* MCHA; NRI.
                           Wooden Pegs from the Lyman Wight Home in Adam-ondi-Ahman. RLDSLA.
                           Partial Window Pane from a Nauvoo Home. RTF.
                           Plaster from a Nauvoo Home. RTF.

DEATH AND BURIAL

Page 56   *The Nauvoo Expositor.* MCHA.
                           Joseph Smith's and Hyrum Smith's Pistols. MCHA.
                           Alvin Smith's Tombstone. LDS Church Archives.
                           Stephen Markham's Cane. MCHA.

Page 57   *The Carthage Jail Door.* VRL.
                           John Taylor's Watch. LDS Church Archives.
                           Hyrum Smith's Blood-Stained Shirt. Eldred G. Smith Family Collection.
                           Mob Member's Powder Horn. MCHA.
                           Hyrum Smith's and Joseph Smith's Death Masks. MCHA.
                           1844 Martyrdom Sampler. MCHA.

PHOTOGRAPHY AND ART

Page 58   *Daguerreotype (Copy) of the City of Nauvoo by Lucian Foster.* LDS Church Archives.
                           1842 American Photographic Camera. George Eastman House, International Museum of Photography, Rochester, New York.

Page 59   *Sketch of the Prophet Joseph Smith.* VRL.
                           Original Daguerreotype Plate of Eliza R. Snow. LDS Church Archives.
                           Richards Family Silhouettes. Private possession.
                           Painting of Joseph Knight, Sr. MCHA.

PIONEERS AND TRAILS

Page 60   *Handcart Used by Mormon Pioneers.* MCHA.

Brigham Young's Compass. MCHA.
Heber C. Kimball's Pioneer Journal. LDS Church Archives.
Oxen Yoke. MCHA.

Page 61 *John Young's Flour Sack.* MCHA.
Orson Pratt's Telescope and Theodolyte with Box. MCHA.
Brass Bucket. MCHA.
Brigham Young's Wagon. DUP.
J. McAllister's Wooden Leg. MCHA.
Thomas Bullock's Pioneer Company Journal. MCHA.

SECTION THREE
THE DOCTRINE AND COVENANTS IN CHURCH HISTORY

Page 63 *1835 Doctrine and Covenants.* HBLLBYU.

Page 64 *David White Rogers's Painting of Joseph Smith (ca. 1842).* MCHA.

THE DEVELOPMENT OF THE DOCTRINE AND COVENANTS

Page 67 **The Evening and the Morning Star.** HBLLBYU.

Page 68 *Unpublished Revelation of Joseph Smith (20 March 1832).* HBLLBYU.

Page 69 *Manuscript Copy of Doctrine and Covenants 64.* RLDSLA.
1833 Book of Commandments. RLDSLA.
Letter from Oliver Cowdery to Bishop Whitney (4 February 1835).
   HBLLBYU.

Page 70 *1835 Doctrine and Covenants.* HBLLBYU.
Broadside of the First Lecture of the Lectures on Faith. HBLLBYU.

Page 71 *1844 Doctrine and Covenants.* HBLLBYU.
1876 Doctrine and Covenants. HBLLBYU.

Page 72 *1921 Doctrine and Covenants.* HBLLBYU.
1981 Doctrine and Covenants. HBLLBYU.

COMMANDMENTS IN THE DOCTRINE AND COVENANTS

Page 73 **United States Senate and Congressional Documents.** Private possession, Greg
   Christofferson, Irvine, California.
1834 Anti-Mormon Book, Mormonism Unvailed. HBLLBYU.

Page 74 *1845 Proclamation.* Private possession, R. Q. Shupe, Capistrano, California.
Share Certificate in the Half-Breed Land Company. LDS Church Archives.

THE JOSEPH SMITH TRANSLATION AND THE DOCTRINE AND COVENANTS

Page 75   *Joseph Smith's 1828 Bible.* RLDSLA.

Page 76   *Joseph Smith's Marked Bible, Pages 746–47 (Revelation, Chapters 7–10).*
           RLDSLA.
           Joseph Smith Translation Manuscripts. RLDSLA.

GEOGRAPHIC LOCATIONS OF THE REVELATIONS

Page 80   *Smith Home in Manchester, New York.* Margaret Rich, ca. 1910.

Page 86   *John Johnson Home, Hiram, Ohio.* Western Reserve Historical Society, before
           1874. Western Reserve Historical Society, Cleveland, Ohio.

Page 89   *Liberty Jail, Liberty, Missouri.* RLDSLA, 1905.

Page 90   *Edward Hunter Home, Nauvoo, Illinois.* Special Collections, J. Willard
           Marriott Library, University of Utah, Salt Lake City, Utah.

Page 91   *Manuscript of John Taylor's 1882 Revelation.* HBLLBYU.

Page 92   *1888 Swedish Doctrine and Covenants with John Taylor's Revelation.*
           HBLLBYU.
           1890 Manifesto Pamphlet. HBLLBYU.

Page 93   *James E. Talmage's Diary Entry for 31 October 1918.* HBLLBYU.
           First Presidency Letter (8 June 1978). HBLLBYU.